A SHORT HISTORY OF WALES

(Overleaf) Tintern Abbey by J. M. Turner

A Short History of WALES

Welsh Life and Customs
from prehistoric times to the present day

A. H. DODD

JOHN JONES

A Short History of Wales © A. H. Dodd

First published by Batsford 1972 as *Life in Wales*
Second impression (paperback) 1977. Reprinted 1990.

This new edition published by John Jones Publishing Ltd, April 1998
Reprinted November 1998
Reprinted November 2007
Reprinted March 2013

ISBN 978-1-871083-36-1

Cover photographs by John Idris Jones.
Cover designed and book printed by Cambrian Printers Ltd,
Aberystwyth, Ceredigion

Published by John Jones Publishing Ltd,
Borthwen, Ruthin, LL15 1DA

Foreword

Arthur Herbert Dodd (1891-1975) was a native of Wrexham and was educated at Grove Park Grammar School in that town and at New College, Oxford. After service in the First World War and a spell in the Civil Service he joined the Department of History at the University College of North Wales, Bangor in 1922; in 1930 he succeeded the founding father of Welsh historical studies, Sir John Edward Lloyd, as professor. He retired in 1958.

Arthur Dodd's first field of interest was the Industrial Revolution in north Wales and this was the title of his first book, published in 1933; this highly detailed book, based on a very wide range of original sources, is regarded as a classic. He then turned his attention to the early modern period; having accepted a commission to write a short book on seventeenth-century Wales, he realised that there was a great deal of basic research to be done before such a book could be written. The result was a series of substantial articles on the part played by Welsh members of the House of Commons after the extension of parliamentary representation to Wales in 1536, on the Civil War in the different counties of north Wales and on numerous other aspects of the social and political history of Tudor and Stuart Wales. He was one of the first historians to see the potential of the great collections of family and estate papers in the National Library of Wales at Aberystwyth and the University Library at Bangor and in *Studies in Stuart Wales* (1952) he added significantly to our understanding of that period.

But his interests were not restricted to Wales. Visits to the USA led him to investigate the pattern of early Welsh emigration across the Atlantic. Lectures to his own students at Bangor resulted in *The Growth of Responsible Government* (1956). In 1961 he published *Life in Elizabethan England* for the Batsford English Life series and in 1972 this was followed by the present volume, originally titled *Life in Wales* and reprinted as *A Short History of Wales* in 1977. In both the spoken and the written word he excelled; he was a particularly lively and elegant lecturer and the same qualities come across in everything he published.

This book illustrates the breadth of Arthur Dodd's scholarship. Although he is best remembered for his work on the early modern period, he had something worth-while to say on most aspects of the history of Wales. It is not a definitive history; he would have been disappointed if it were seen in this light, since no historian can ever say the last word. But it is a useful and eminently readable introduction for those who would like to know more about the country and its people and it ranges from the earliest evidence of human settlement on Welsh soil to the 1960s. Nothing is omitted; emergence of Wales, the coming of the Normans, the age of the native princes, the revolt of Owain Glyn Dŵr, Henry Tudor's march to Bosworth, the Acts of Union, the Methodist revival, the coming of large-scale industry – all are here, and much else besides. The last thirty years have seen a flowering of Welsh historical studies. It is fair to say that Arthur Dodd was one of those who sowed the seeds and his work has been carried on by many of his pupils. Some readers may be drawn to try to find out more about some of the topics included in this book; to this end a short bibliography of works published since 1972 has been added to supplement the original bibliographies included at the end of each chapter.

Professors are often perceived as remote and austere figures but in no way could these adjectives ever have been applied to Arthur Dodd. Throughout his life he was active in the field of adult education and for many years he was responsible for this aspect of his university's activity; in many ways this book reflects that experience. He lectured indefatigably to societies and organisations of all kinds all over north Wales. He was a natural communicator; he never patronised or talked down to his students, his listeners or his readers and to his students he was universally held not only in respect but in affection. These qualities are manifest in *A Short History of Wales* and it is a book which can be read with enjoyment as well as profit. It is worth remembering that it is the work of a man who had entered his ninth decade when he wrote it and it has about it that sense of mellow reflection which stems from years of thought and study. For the visitor to Wales who wants to learn something of a nation's experience there can be no better introduction.

A. D. CARR
Reader in Welsh History
University of Wales
Bangor

Preface

The author wishes to express his personal thanks to the officials of the National Library, the National Museum, and the University College Library, Bangor, for their unfailing help at every stage of the work; he is particularly grateful to the Librarian's secretary at Bangor, Mrs Parry, who readily made herself responsible for the typing, and to Mrs Rachel Bromwich, of Cambridge, and Mr Robin Livens, of Bangor, who read through the early pages in draft and offered many suggestions which were adopted with advantage.

Contents

Acknowledgment

The author and publishers wish to thank the following for the illustrations appearing in this book:

Aerofilms Ltd. for page 148(b); Anglesey Antiquarian Society for page 114; the Trustees of the British Museum for pages 20(b), 91, 128, 135 and 154; the British Tourist Authority for pages 50 and 92 (b); Cardiff Public Libraries for page 124; Cambrian Archaeological Association for pages 3, 49 and 82; the Hon. Society of Cymmrodorion for pages 20(a) and 28; Denbighshire Historical Society for page 151; Honoria Durant and the Duke of Beaufort for pages 90 and 92(a); *The Glamorgan Historian* and D. Brown and Sons, Cowbridge, for pages 113(a) and (b); the Historical Society of Pennsylvania for page 95; the Mansell Collection for pages 64, 76(a) and 126; the Ministry of Public Building and Works for page 34; Museum of Welsh Antiquities, Bangor, for pages 16(b), 133 and 152; National Library of Wales for pages 29, 37, 38, 63, 74, 76(b), 77, 86, 99, 106, 115, 117(b), 120, 140, 143 and 157; the National Museum of Wales for pages 2, 5, 6, 8, 10, 13, 14, 15, 22, 45, 104, 108, 117, 118, 122 and 158; National Monuments Record for pages 24, 28, 51 and 134; W. and O. Pritchard, Llanfairpwll, and the Dalkeith Press, Kettering, for page 123; *Punch* for page 156; Radio Times Hulton Picture Library for page 162; Rev. M. Ridgway for pages 47 and 71; Royal Commission on Ancient Monuments in Wales and Monmouthshire for pages 9, 11, 23, 41, 54 and 67; Society of Antiquaries, London, for page 4; Victoria and Albert Museum for page 53.

The Illustrations

I

The Earliest Inhabitants

Towards the end of the eighth century AD, King Offa of Mercia built the dyke extending, intermittently, for nearly 150 miles, which still approximates to the existing frontier between England and Wales. Forty years ago a distinguished archaeologist asked a Montgomeryshire countryman through whose garden it passed, if its origin and purpose were still understood by the local inhabitants. 'You put your head inside the back-door of Bob Jones's cottage there,' was the reply; 'tell him he was born the wrong side of Offa's Dyke, and see what happens.'

Bob Jones's scorn has roots far deeper in history than the building of Offa's dyke. For countless ages the land between Offa's frontier and the sea had been swept by successive waves of prospectors and settlers, each following lines determined by the physical lay-out of the country, and all combining to produce the Welsh people. Westward lay a long and exposed coastline, with projecting arms in Llŷn and Pembrokeshire and frequent indentations which invited the invader from Ireland or Spain or Brittany; eastward the main river valleys, as well as the southern coastal plain, lay open to incursions from the English lowlands. Broken though the country is, geography has given it a certain natural unity and a natural frontier—the palaeozoic outcrops underlying Offa's engineering feat. Within these bounds successive cultures have been absorbed and adapted till there emerged a heritage stubbornly cherished in the teeth even of military conquest.

Apart from a few fragments of debatable age, the earliest known inhabitant of the area was the mysterious being mistakenly christened the Red Lady of Paviland by the archaeo-

Paviland cave, Gower

logist who made the discovery, nearly a century and a half ago. The Red Lady turned out, on later examination, to be a young man who left his ochre-stained bones, along with sundry ornaments and tools and the bones of contemporary beasts, in the Goat's Hole cave at Paviland in Gower, before the final retreat of the ice-sheets from Britain. Similar traces of early human life have turned up in other Welsh caves, none of them far inland. The remains are those of hunters who were not equipped with tools to enable them to penetrate the interior, but lived on what they could hunt down where they first found shelter. These earliest inhabitants may well have been swept away by the return of Arctic conditions; certainly they left nothing behind them to enrich posterity.

2

After the final retreat of the ice, some eight thousand years before the Christian era, a moister and warmer climate began to cover the land with trees and to create an environment suitable to horse, ox and pig instead of mammoth and reindeer. These conditions attracted fresh immigrants from the continent bringing with them more advanced techniques for fashioning flint and chert into tools, which gave them greater control over nature and began to turn them into true colonists rather than solitary and sporadic food-gatherers. But flint and chert are far from abundant in Wales, and these settlers were few and scattered; they rarely reached the uplands, which remained the haunt of wild beasts.

Up to this point the advance of 'civilization' had been slow and halting. But in the course of the third and early second millennia before Christ there set in a much more fundamental and rapid transformation in social life, achieving more in centuries than had been accomplished before in millennia. This new civilization—the Neolithic—was brought to Wales by successive groups originating round the shores of the Mediterranean, and bringing with them the more developed arts of that area. They were short, dark, long-headed folk,

Bryn Celli Ddu chambered tomb (Anglesey), as it appeared in 1847

Pentre Ifan Megalithic tomb

known to earlier generations of anthropologists as Iberians. Some landed from France along the South Wales coast, others came from Spain or Brittany to Ireland, whence a short hop brought them to the western tips of modern Caernarvonshire or Pembrokeshire.

They came to a thinly-populated land, in quest of pastures and cornfields (for they had learned to domesticate animals and to sow crops), and possibly of ores too. As their very migrations show, they were hardy, adventurous and mobile; they were also skilful engineers, witness their impressive megalithic monuments, which have been described as 'stone-built family vaults for the upper ranks of society', though time and tillage have often worn them down to those gaunt skeletons familiar to us as cromlechs. With the exception of a few settlements in the Black Mountains of Breconshire the Neolithic invaders were plainsmen, and made little contribution towards peopling the mountainous hinterland.

4

Like so many primitive peoples, they seem to have lavished greater care on housing their dead than their living, for few relics of their habitations have survived. On the other hand it was they who introduced Wales not only to the rudiments of agriculture, but to those of trade and manufacture too. Of this the best example is the axe factory at Graig Lwyd, on Penmaenmawr, which reveals a substantial measure of organization and specialization and of an overland trade extending the length and breadth of Wales and as far south as Wiltshire.

A fresh series of migrations, spread over some thousand years from the middle of the second millennium BC brought new arts to Wales. The invaders came mainly from central and eastern Europe, and their main contribution was the use of bronze for tools and of bronze and gold for personal adornment. Welsh ores were not yet brought into play to any significant extent; the tin came from Cornwall, the copper and gold mainly from Ireland or the continent. Heavier tools with a better cutting edge, and possibly an improvement in the climate, giving access to wider pastures, led to a deeper penetration. Trade routes were extended and used by travelling craftsmen from Ireland and from southern England; but the new skills were gradually acquired in Wales itself, and developed into many distinctive local styles. The heaviest concentration and the most advanced developments were in south-eastern Wales, with its agricultural and pastoral wealth.

Bronze age pottery, Llandow Glamorganshire

Social organization was clearly advancing, but of domestic life in Bronze Age Wales we still know little, apart from what can be learnt from the food vessels and cinerary urns provided for the dead, who were buried

Bronze age cauldron from Llyn Fawr, Glamorgan

in individual graves, often marked by massive standing stones and with every sign of elaborate ritual. Cremation, by no means unknown in Neolithic Wales, became a universal practice from about 800 BC. In the nature of things, the spread of culture can have owed little to migratory peasants; it was the wealth of their warlords that made possible the importation and manufacture of luxury goods. The Bronze Age folk were sometimes content to live in empty Stone Age caves; if they built for themselves, their structures were too flimsy to survive. Habits were no doubt still largely nomadic.

We know no more of the language spoken by the Bronze Age folk than we do of what their predecessors used, unless some relic of it can be traced in the Basque tongue. But their successors, the Celts, with whom the Iron Age dawned in Britain, brought with them an Indo-European tongue which in its two branches of Brythonic (or British) and Goidelic (or Gaelic), is the basis of the language still spoken in Wales, Brittany, Ireland and the Scottish highlands and islands. The cradle of the Celts lay between the middle Rhine and Upper Danube, but from about 600 BC they were spreading outwards, carrying with them their knowledge of iron. Their arrival in Britain cannot have been much later than 500 BC and they came in successive batches over a period of some five hundred

6

years, some making the short trip across the Straits of Dover, others the more adventurous passage from Brittany to Ireland or western Scotland, Wales or the west of England.

The Celts were a warlike people, skilled in the use of the best contemporary weapons and organized in tribes under a warrior aristocracy. They were thus able to overrun the country and to reduce its existing inhabitants to subjection. During their continental migrations they had enriched their native culture by contact with Hellenic and other advanced civilizations, and had developed highly sophisticated art forms; once again these products soon came to be manufactured, with many regional variations, in their new homeland.

The invaders had their religious as well as their military leaders. Much has been written about the Druids, but little is known with any certainty. It appears that the cult of lakes and rivers entered largely into their worship, precious votive offerings being cast in to propitiate the gods; and although in Britain they remained in touch with the Druids of Gaul, Anglesey became an important local centre for their religion. What we know of domestic life is derived mainly from the defended settlements—rather misleadingly called 'hill forts'—which Iron Age man constructed in positions of natural strength. Here, under the protection of defensive earthen walls, reinforced with timber, stones and boulders, normal life was carried on in communities ranging from villages of several hundred inhabitants to single households.

Within the ramparts, and sometimes spreading beyond them, were circular huts, built of timber or wattle on stone foundations. The threat of tribal war or of fresh invasion was never far off, calling for periodic reconstruction, and even occasional desertion, of the site; but normally its natural strength was enough to ward off intruders. It is extremely rare, at any period before the coming of the Romans, to find any clear evidence of fighting round a 'hill fort'. For most purposes life within was self-contained. Daily necessities like food, clothing and tools were produced on the spot, and many of the sites were extensive enough to accommodate flocks and herds. What had to be procured outside was bought by barter: the coinage in daily use in south-eastern Britain seems to have

7

Bronze torque, Llyn Cerrig Bach, Anglesey   *Caergwrle bowl*

been virtually unknown in the remoter and more backward west.

Such was the Wales that confronted the Roman legions when, having subdued the English lowlands between AD 43 and 47, they were faced with the task of pursuing the most intrepid of the southern 'kings', Caratacus (or Caradog), into the western highlands, where he was organizing resistance. The social pattern was looser here than in the more settled regions of eastern and southern Britain. There was no powerful combination like the Brigantes or Boudicca's Iceni—only a number of small local tribes and a few wider groups like the Silures in the south and the Ordovices in the north; and no unifying force unless it came from the Druidical religion. On the other hand nature presented formidable barriers to the Roman, as to many later invaders. A hill-top village could not be overrun by a cavalry charge, and the western tribes clung fiercely to their independence.

By AD 51 Caradog had been defeated and captured, but it took another generation to subdue the Silures; in fact it would appear that the tribe was virtually wiped out in the struggle. Among the Ordovices a Roman force, leaving many of the hill tribes still unconquered or only partially subdued, moved into Anglesey in AD 60 to make an end of the Druids. There followed a wholesale massacre of these troublemakers and the destruction of their sacred groves. There may be some reflection of this crisis in the rich deposit of Iron Age metalwork, mainly warlike but including specimens of Celtic art at its finest, which was discovered in the peaty margin of a lake in south-western Anglesey some thirty years ago. The latest finds belong approximately to the age of the Roman invasion of the island; the earliest to a couple of centuries earlier. They are not of local workmanship, but originated in many distant parts of Britain. It has been suggested that they were votive offerings cast into the lake rather than mere spoils of war.

Before this, the work had begun of constructing strong legionary fortresses at Deva (Chester) and Isca (Caerleon) to contain the western tribes. These were linked by fine military roads, which were later extended by branch roads serving auxiliary forts and marching camps as far west as Segontium (Caernarvon) in the north and Moridunum (Carmarthen) in the south. The two great western promontories and (once the Druids had been wiped out) even the isle of Anglesey remained virtually outside the Roman sphere of influence, and in close touch with Ireland, which the Romans never invaded.

Holyhead hut group

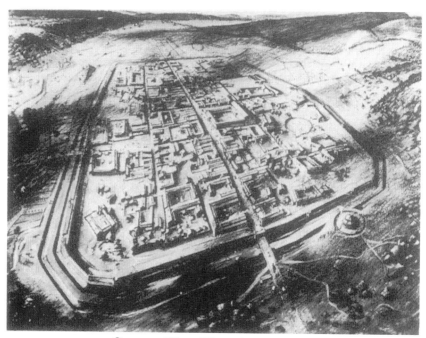

Caerwent (Venta Silurum), reconstruction

Within these limits the conquest of Wales was completed by
AD 80, and for some three centuries it remained an integral
part of the Roman system, making its contributions in man-
power and in kind to the occupying power. The Celtic aristocracy, in the regions under effective rule, became largely
'Romanized', proud of its Roman citizenship and at home in
the language of the conquerors and their methods of civil
government. In the south-east, where the process was most
complete, there appeared a Roman town, Caerwent, with all
the familiar paraphernalia of Roman urban life. Along the
southern plain were several *villae*—houses built after the Roman
style, surrounded by small estates or farms and inhabited by
Romanized Britons of wealth and standing. Smaller settlements and hamlets which have been uncovered here and there
also give evidence of occupation by natives with Romanized
habits. But Roman rule in Wales was mainly military, and the
farther west and north one looks, the thinner the Roman
veneer becomes. Current excavations at Carmarthen, how-

ever, are bringing to light the existence of a civil settlement much farther west than hitherto thought.

Rome wanted corn from her new province, and there are signs that agriculture was extended and improved. From time to time groups of native farm buildings, or more extensive settlements, of the Roman period, are turned up by the archaeologist's spade; and one of the lasting domestic legacies was the use of the rotary quern instead of the primitive saddle quern for grinding corn. Rome also wanted metals, and there is plenty of evidence of the working of Wales's neglected ores, with native settlements at hand to supply the labour force.

From the fourth century, Rome was unable to give effective protection to the western approaches, which had never really entered into her defensive system; for it is clear that Anglesey and the western promontories were increasingly subject to predatory raids and to permanent settlement from across the Irish Sea. The reoccupation of some of the deserted 'hill forts' testifies to Rome's weakening grip, and reveals her increasing readiness to entrust the natives with their own defence. There were other threats to Roman power. In the north the province was under frequent attack from Pictish raiders, on the east and south from Saxon pirates; on the continent mass movements

Hut from Romano-British village (Din Lligwy, Anglesey)

among the barbarian peoples, and recurrent civil wars, drained the Welsh garrisons for service elsewhere.

In AD 383 Magnus Maximus, a soldier of Spanish origin stationed here, was acclaimed emperor by the army in Britain. He crossed with his followers to Gaul, where he maintained himself as emperor of the western provinces for five years, until he was defeated and slain in Italy. His army never returned; some from the neighbourhood of Segontium appear in an army list in a remote part of the empire a few years later. This lends some colour to the tradition that he had married a Segontian wife, and to the claim of some of the Welsh dynasties that they were descendants of Maximus (the Macsen Wledig of Welsh tradition) and his wife Helen—a name long revered in Wales. This was the end of Roman military rule there, although it survived a little longer in the rest of the island. It may well be that Maximus had made some arrangement for the interim government, in his absence, of the Welsh Roman province through native magnates. If so, what remained the pattern of political life had already been sketched out before the legionaries left.

Further Reading

General:

A. J. Roderick (ed.), *Wales through the Ages* (2 vols.), 1959 and 1960.

W. Rees, *Historical Atlas of Wales*, 1951.

T. Parry (trans. H. I. Bell), *History of Welsh Literature*, 1955.

J. W. James, *Church History of Wales*, 1945.

Chapter I:

J. E. Lloyd (ed.), *A Hundred Years of Welsh Archaeology*, 1946.

W. F. Grimes, *The Prehistory of Wales* (2nd ed.), 1951.

L. Alcock, 'Celtic archaeology and art', in *Celtic Studies in Wales* (ed. Elwyn Davies), 1963.

V. E. Nash Williams, *The Roman Frontier in Wales*, 1954.

R. E. Mortimer Wheeler, *Roman Archaeology in Wales* (B.B.C. lecture), 1957.

Stuart Piggott, *The Druids*, 1966.

G. E. Daniel and I. Foster, *Prehistoric and Early Wales*, 1963.

II

Cymry, Teutons and Normans

With the departure of Macsen Wledig, the curtain tem-
porarily falls on life in Wales. Most of the legionary and
auxiliary fortresses soon became derelict. Venta Silurum, the
only considerable urban centre, was no longer a seat of civil
government, although until the middle of the fifth century a
dwindling population squatted among its decaying buildings.
Money no longer circulated, what little trade remained being
carried on by barter. Tillage appears to have receded, and
the mining of metals slackened or ceased. The Roman roads
disintegrated into mere horse tracks, with
grass encroaching on the margins. The
making of any but the crudest pottery also
petered out.

*Penannular brooch
from Anglesey
(6th century)*

Yet there is another side to the picture.
Seaboard Wales has always tended to look
westward rather than eastward, forming
one limit of 'the cultural community of
the Irish Sea Zone'. And the western
seaways were still open to travelling craftsmen, who helped to maintain something
of a common culture. Apart from the
highly developed Irish crafts, luxuries
from Gaul and even from the Mediterranean could find their way to remote
fastnesses like Dinas Powys in the south
or Dinas Emrys in the north: wines and
oil and the latest products of continental
craftsmanship in silverware and glassware

13

Homestead, Anglesey (reconstruction)

—and this for chieftains living in what to Roman eyes would seem barbaric state, in buildings of timber and unmortared stone, with never a bath house to relieve the squalor. At Dinas Powys, at least, there is evidence that local craftsmen could produce their own versions of these luxury goods. Along these same seaways Christianity returned to Wales. The empire had been officially Christian since early in the fourth century, and Isca Silurum is believed to have provided martyrs to the faith even earlier. Macsen Wledig was reputed a Christian, but there is no evidence that these religious influences had spread beyond the official classes and the more Romanized areas. In the countryside the local Celtic cults remained intact, with some admixture of imported Roman and even oriental religious fashions like the worship of Mithras, whose temple at Segontium was in use throughout the third century.

Early in the fifth century, missionaries from Gaul began to turn their attention to their fellow Celts of Britain, and before its close Illtud introduced Celtic monasticism from the continent, and established (traditionally at Llanilltud Fawr, or Llantwit Major, in Glamorgan) a school which became both a seat of continental learning and a missionary centre. Still wider was the fame, as ascetic and preacher, of Dewi (or St David), whose monastery in Pembrokeshire eventually superseded Llantwit.

Politically the age was one of disintegration. The Roman occupation had undermined tribal cohesion, and the only shred of authority left was what could be exercised locally by men of valour, wealth or high descent. Many of these were Romanized Britons who still claimed to act under imperial authority and flaunted imperial titles. Before Macsen Wledig left the country, an Irish Christian tribe settled in Pembrokeshire under its chieftain; five generations later, his descendant still ruled there and used the same Roman title.

The situation was different in the north. Here the Irish settlements were merely scattered groups, numerous enough to introduce their Goidelic tongue into Anglesey and the Llŷn peninsula, but not cohesive enough to form the basis of a political unit, and apparently untouched by Roman and Christian influences. The scene was transformed by the arrival of Cunedda and his tribe of the Votadini (or Gododdin) from north of the Roman Wall. The invaders had evidently come under strong Roman and Christian influences, and felt themselves to stand for Roman civilization. With their superior organization they established their ascendancy in north-western Wales, which emerged in the course of the next century as the realm of Gwynedd. Cunedda's sons and successors extended their conquests as far south as the Teifi, leaving their names to the modern Welsh counties of Cardigan and

Voteporex stone

Maen Achwyfan stone cross, near Whitford (Flintshire)

Merioneth as well as to some of the smaller divisions. During the same period other Welsh dynasties were establishing themselves elsewhere, and the Brythonic tongue was ousting the Goidelic.

With the conquerors came the missionaries, some in the train of Cunedda, some from the Christianized regions of the south. It was an aristocratic movement, with many of the missionaries or 'saints' claiming relationship with the conquering families. Some lived as hermits, some gathered round them a group of disciples living in huts which (to judge from the few surviving remains) were not unlike those of the traditional Celtic village; and from such centres, disciples would set out on further missions, to establish similar communities up and down the land.

The new society emerging during the sixth century could rightly be called Romano-British. The Roman influences which had not penetrated deeply during the military occupa-

First known writing in Welsh, c. 700 AD

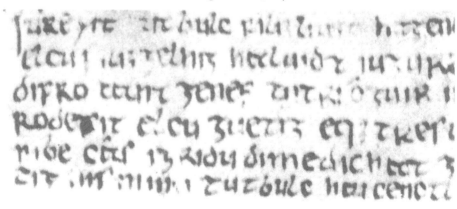

tion now became diffused through the influence of the Church. There was a brisk interchange of scholars between Christian Gaul and Christian Britain. Memorial stones of the fifth and sixth centuries, with Latin inscriptions, testify to a society which had doctors and magistrates as well as princes and priests. By the middle of the sixth century the Welsh language was evolving out of the primitive British tongue, becoming a flexible medium for the oral transmission of heroic verse, primitive folk tales, pedigrees and other tribal memorabilia.

Inevitably there were tensions between the Latin and Celtic elements; for example, the sixth-century British monk Gildas denounced the 'barbarism' of contemporary Welsh princes, especially their susceptibility to the flatteries of court poets. The new religious forces brought with them a fresh crop of words—this time from literary Latin—to join those which had filtered in during the military occupation; but Welsh remained the language of daily intercourse, Latin for legal and liturgical uses only. Even here it soon ceased to have the field entirely to itself. The earliest known piece of written Welsh, dating from about the end of the eighth century, appears in a Latin copy of the Gospels now preserved in Lichfield cathedral. It records the settlement of a dispute about land; but the writer's Latin gives out, and has to be padded out with the vernacular.

Meanwhile the Teutonic settlements in eastern Britain were pressing steadily westwards, so that the Britons of the western highlands became conscious of themselves as sole heirs of the Romano-British civilization. As the pressure increased, successive bands of emigrants left the western Celtic fringe of Britain for Armorica, now renamed Brittany. Throughout the sixth century the constant interchange (chiefly of missionaries) between these regions, which followed much the same routes as those of the contemporary traders—or for that matter of the traders of prehistoric days—tended to strengthen Celtic rather than Latin influences.

The most intimate contacts of the 'Welsh', as the Germanic invaders learned to call them, were naturally with their blood-brothers the 'Men of the North', with whom they shared a wealth of common tradition and a close similarity of language. The bonds were drawn tighter by the desperate struggle in the early years of the seventh century for supremacy in northern Britain, in the course of which they came to call themselves Cymry, or compatriots. It must have been in the first flush of Cymric victories that a memorial—now preserved in the little Anglesey church of Llangadwaladr—was put up by Cadwaladr, the victor's son, commemorating his grandfather Cadfan in grandiloquent terms borrowed from a Byzantine court formula. But retribution came swiftly. By the middle of the seventh century Teutonic supremacy had been established in North Britain. The Welsh were now cut off from their fellow-Cymry, save for religious contacts, and linguistic ties which may have lingered on till the Norman Conquest. Long before that the Mercian king, Offa, had pushed Mercian conquests farther west and then built his 150-mile dyke to mark a frontier evidently arrived at by treaty.

In the visual arts the Welsh lagged sadly behind the Irish.

Offa's Dyke, near Brymbo, Denbighshire

But at least the wheel-crosses at Carew or Nevern in Pembrokeshire, at Whitland in Flintshire or Penmon in Anglesey, with their intricate, interlaced patterns, show that native craftsmen had not entirely lost their cunning in the characteristic motifs of Celtic art up to the eve of the Norman conquest.

By the middle of the ninth century, Cymru had become a distinct country and the Cymry a distinct people. They were also achieving some political unity as one dynasty after another succeeded, by marriage or conquest, in establishing supremacy over its neighbours; but never with the finality of the West Saxon overlordship which ended by unifying England, if only because Welsh custom did not admit primogeniture. Regional consciousness also remained strong. 'Cymru' was a concept belonging to the sphere of language and culture rather than politics; politically what mattered was Gwynedd or Powys, Dyfed or Deheubarth.

There were other signs of consolidation among the Welsh, such as a growing awareness of and pride in their own history. Before the end of the eighth century the monks of St Davids were jotting down contemporary Latin annals which became the foundation documents for the history of Wales in its years of independence. There followed the more ambitious *History of the Britons* compiled in Latin about 800 by the otherwise unknown Welsh monk Nennius—a fantastic mixture of half-digested Latin book-learning and popular myth translated from oral sources in Welsh.

This combination of a rising standard of political organization and patriotic sentiment with cultural standards which suggest isolation and inbreeding is not surprising. About the middle of the ninth century there began the series of Viking raids into Europe which continued sporadically till the Norman Conquest. Ireland and the Isle of Man were the bases from which the raiders swooped down to burn and loot Welsh monasteries and churches, and occasionally to establish trading bases by the coast, as at Tenby, Bardsey or the Orme. On the whole, however, the contribution of the Norsemen to the racial stock or the cultural heritage of Wales is negligible. Their influence was mainly negative. They largely cut Wales off from Ireland and western Europe, which had been such in-

Pilgrim effigy in Llandyfodwg Church Pembrokeshire

Silver penny of Hywel Dda

vigorating influences until the end of the seventh century. The importation of objects of fine craftsmanship ceased; literary contacts faded. The chief positive effect was to hasten the development of common political consciousness and of political ties with England for the common defence.

The invasions may also have helped to break down religious isolation. During the break-up of the western Roman Empire the Celtic Church had been largely cut off from Latin Christendom, and had developed or retained practices which came to be cherished for their own sake. The common threat to Christendom helped to blunt these prejudices, and in 768 the Welsh Church brought itself, outwardly at least, into conformity with the usages of western Christendom. As a result pilgrimages became common, one of the most significant being one to Rome, about 930, by Hywel Dda, who claimed to be king of all Wales and effectively ruled all but the south-east. He is the first Welsh ruler known to have issued his own coinage; at the same time he recognized, in general, the overlordship of Wessex.

Later tradition ascribes to Hywel the 'codification' of Welsh law. The earliest copies of the supposed 'code' were written at least three centuries later, but they contain many pointers to practices of the age of Hywel himself. Like most societies emerging from the chaos that followed the collapse of Rome, Welsh society was a broad-based pyramid. At the top came the ruler, whether of a single *gwlad* or territory, or of most of Wales. Then came the various degrees of notables (*uchelwyr*) and freemen (*priodorion*), owing him services compatible with their rank, and with rights in the grazing and arable which were exercised individually but

20

held for the entire *cenedl* or kin group. The base of the pyramid was the bondsmen—descendants, no doubt, of conquered populations reduced to servitude in the successive invasions, and far outnumbering the freemen. Their status, too, showed wide variations. All were attached to the soil, some so closely that they could be sold with it like the other livestock, when alienation became possible. Many were huddled into bond hamlets clustered around the lord's *llys*. Here they raised his crops, guarded his flocks from marauders, and laboured to build or repair the *llys*.

In the dearth of datable remains it is hard to be positive about housing. Some of the homesteads whose foundations periodically come to light, suggesting rectangular drystone or timber structures round courtyards, terraces for cultivation, and low enclosing walls, may indicate the homes of *uchelwyr* of the first millennium AD; and similarly the more lightly-built groups of circular hut foundations, which are thick on the ground in some regions, may have been bond settlements. But these latter are ready victims to agricultural advance, and generally survive only where the land is too poor to be worth clearing, whilst the superior houses often lie buried under their more pretentious successors.

The death of Hywel in 950 put an end to the precarious unity he had built on foundations laid by his grandfather Rhodri Mawr. Between his death and the Norman Conquest approximately thirty-five Welsh rulers were killed by Saxons or Danes or fellow-Welshmen. William the Conqueror had by 1070 made himself master of England and was ready to attack the disunited Welsh. The task was initially entrusted to his followers, whom he had established in earldoms at Chester, Shrewsbury and Hereford. From these bases they advanced along the historic routes, fortifying themselves as they went by building 'motte-and-bailey' castles. These were high conical mounds surmounted by wooden towers and encircled with palisades, with a similarly protected courtyard annexed. They were often replaced by masonry castles in the following two centuries.

Before the end of the eleventh century the Norman invaders had penetrated South Wales as far as Pembroke, the valleys

Norman castle, Pembroke

of Central Wales to Cardigan Bay and the coast of North Wales as far as Anglesey; the mountainous core of the land still remained beyond their reach. Then the Welsh rallied. The rightful heir to Gwynedd, Gruffydd ap Cynan, who had been born in exile among his mother's Norse relations in Ireland, made three successive bids for his inheritance, and on the third succeeded. By the time he died in 1137 he had not only recovered most of it but, according to his anonymous biographer who wrote later in the century, he enabled his exhausted subjects once more to 'support themselves from the fruit of the earth after the fashion of the Romans'—a striking testimony to the way *pax Romana* lingered on in folk memory as a golden age. Opposition to the Normans never reached a national scale, since Norman kings could always find allies among Welsh princes: but the resistance of Gwynedd was upheld by a succession of able rulers, despite punitive expeditions by Rufus and Henry II. All that was achieved was a vague recognition of the feudal overlordship of the English crown, symbolized by the abandonment of the title 'king' and the substitution of 'lord'.

This applied also to the other Welsh rulers. The last ruler of Powys to call himself 'king' died in 1160; his successors were in effect feudal barons, ruling a much diminished territory. The last of the kings of Deheubarth, hemmed in by Norman lordships on both flanks, exchanged his title in 1158 for that of 'Lord Rhys', in which capacity he ruled in great splendour as Henry II's 'Justice of South Wales'. Lesser Welsh potentates had to content themselves with petty feudal lordships to which their dominions had shrunk. Yet the Welsh rulers, for all their diminished status, were still able to maintain something of the Welsh way of life; the Lord Rhys, for example, presided in 1176 over a magnificent eisteddfod in Cardigan castle, at which the 'chair' for poetry went to a bard from Gwynedd. It was on lordships like Brecon, Glamorgan or Pembroke, carved out by individual Norman adventurers by piecemeal conquest, that the Norman hand fell heaviest. Here they seized on the best lands and built themselves stone castles in the latest style, where they lorded it almost as independent sovereigns. The native Welsh were relegated to 'Welshries', mainly in the uplands, where they were able to preserve traditional habits and to hold their lands and settle their disputes by Welsh law—subject only to what tribute their alien overlords might impose.

Norman influence was by no means confined to these areas of direct rule. Even in *pura Wallia* Norman ways proved attractive at least among the upper classes. The outward and visible

Norman motte, St Clears castle

Dolwyddelan castle, Caernarvonshire (c. *1170*)

sign is the building of Norman castles by native rulers, for defence either against the new enemy or against each other; at first of the motte-and-bailey type, but from about 1130 onwards rectangular stone keeps. Here they learned to keep up a ceremonial state borrowed no doubt from Norman practice. Lesser residences, even of the more important rulers, would generally be aisled timber halls. Few of these have survived; two were carried off bodily by Edward I on his conquest of Gwynedd, and traces of one are to be found among the ruins of Harlech castle. It at least gives us some idea of the original dimensions: eighteen feet by thirty-seven.

Otherwise almost the only dwellings of which traces have survived from this period are the 'platform houses' built on levelled platforms dug into a sloping hillside. The sites—and generally nothing but the site survives—are widely scattered over Wales in a variety of sizes, suggesting their use by a wide range of social classes. For our scanty evidence on the homes of the peasantry we have to make do with literary sources such as the *Itinerary* and *Description* of Gerald of Wales—Giraldus

Cambrensis. Descended on his mother's side from the last of
the independent princes of South Wales and on his father's
from a Norman family, Gerald was brought up among his
father's people in Normanized Pembrokeshire, but in 1188
he went on a tour of Wales with the archbishop of Canterbury
to recruit for a crusade.

In the *Description* Gerald gives us a vivid picture of the
contemporary Welshman: his love of part-singing and instru-
mental music, his touchiness and family pride, his ready wit
in speech and skill in story-telling, his religious devotion, his
frugality in food and dress; even details like fussiness about his
teeth, the fashion of moustaches and shaven chins among men
and of 'page-boy' hair styles in both sexes. He tells us how the
peasant makes his coracle for fishing, and depicts him walking
backwards, with goad in hand and song on lips, in front of his
plough team of oxen. The *Itinerary*, though equally entertain-
ing, is less informative: the tour, in a circuit which left the
mountainous heartland untouched, took only some six weeks
(barely one of them in North Wales); and when he tells us
that the peasants live in small huts made of plaited boughs,
lasting only a year, it has been suggested that what he really
saw were the temporary shelters (*hafotai*) used by herdsmen
when the cattle went to summer pasture. His strictures on
Welsh farming practices, however, carry the ring of truth:
'only in March and April is the soil turned over for oats'; and
as for diet, 'almost the whole population lives on its flocks and
on oats, milk, cheese and butter'.

Perhaps the most far-reaching effects of the Conquest arose
from the Norman addiction to town life. Norman lords created
new boroughs; Welsh lords followed suit. Towns meant trade,
and trade meant a wider circulation of money. This tended
to undermine the social structure, since it provided an escape
for the bondsman from some of the more hampering conditions
of his servitude, and even from the restriction of his servile
hamlet. At the same time the growing pressure of the free clans
on the land, as the subdivisions of holdings multiplied, called
for an extensive resettlement. Fresh lands were taken under
cultivation, old bond lands encroached upon, and there came
into existence the characteristic Welsh institution of the *gwely*—

a complex of rights over widely-scattered areas of arable and pasture held by a group of free kinsmen and known by the name of the common ancestor. The obligations both to the kin-group and to the *arglwydd* which were inherent in the *gwely* persisted, and helped to hold the clan together, long after the lands themselves had been redistributed individually in the fourth generation. Gradually the number of freemen came to exceed that of the bondsmen, though probably these still constituted something like a third of the whole.

This resettlement, organized by the growing class of Welsh lawyers, facilitated both the collection of dues and the replanting of regions devastated by war. At the same time administrative divisions like the *cymwd* and the newer *cantref* were taking more definite shape, and the lawyers were compiling the law books which went collectively by the name of the Laws of Hywel Dda. These were in fact guides, in Latin or in Welsh, to the pleader in the courts.

It was not only Welsh laws that were reduced to writing and brought up to date. The epic poems transmitted orally since the first emergence of the Cymry now circulated in written form, as did the primitive prose romances and history. The annals which for some four hundred years had been recorded in Welsh monastic communities were continued and multiplied; but a far more ambitious enterprise, which rapidly became a best-seller, was the *Historia Regum Britanniae*, written in 1136 by Geoffrey Arthur, a cleric of Breton origin brought

A Welsh king

Huntsmen

Judge

up in Monmouthshire and best known as Geoffrey of Monmouth.

Geoffrey traces the ancestry of the Welsh to the legendary Brutus the Trojan and carries their story down to the death of the historical Cadwaladr. He certainly drew on some otherwise unknown Celtic sources, but his main standby was his powerful imagination, whether exercised on mere embroidery or on sheer invention. The Welsh naturally lapped up this glorification of their past—judiciously skipping, perhaps, the author's jeremiads on the degeneracy of those who stayed to be conquered instead of carrying their banner unstained to Brittany. Before the end of the thirteenth century a Welsh version had appeared, and others soon followed.

More surprisingly, the *Historia Regum* caught on with the Normans too. The Saxons were a common enemy to both peoples; moreover the story of Arthur was shared as a folk tradition in Brittany, which had also added its quota of adventurers to the Norman invasion. To the Welsh this revived interest in their early beginnings, whether embodied in epic, law, folk tale or what passed for history, was a powerful spur to patriotic sentiment. This appears in the abundant poetry of the age. The *pencerdd*, a sort of poet laureate, figures in the law books as holding one of the most honourable places at court, and each *uchelwr* had his household bard, whose duty it was to recite the family pedigree and to recall ancestral deeds of valour. Some took on themselves the prophetic mantle, fore-

Lovers

Messenger with lance

Weapons

12th century font, Llangristiolus, Anglesey

telling the return of past glories or of past heroes; or, more practically, uttering unheeded advice about restoring the unity of Wales under a single house.

The Norman love of system and order was seen also in the Church. The settlements established by some of the more influential of the sixth-century saints were organized into territorial dioceses. The outlying churches were given a parochial organization defining the area of their cure of souls. The tiny oratory which had served the founder developed into a stone-built church often bearing his name. Yet the local craftsmen who rebuilt these churches often decorated them, till well on in the twelfth century, with the traditional interlaced designs characteristic of the stone crosses their forefathers had erected a couple of centuries before the Normans came.

It was not without a struggle that the newly-defined Welsh dioceses could be brought to conform with the orderly habits of the Normans by subjecting themselves to the metropolitan authority of Canterbury. In the north Owain Gwynedd persuaded the chapter of Bangor to elect as bishop his own

Valle Crucis Abbey, Llangollen

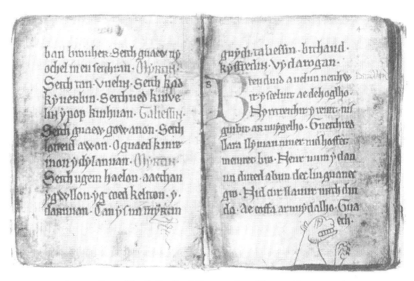

A page from Black Book of Carmarthen (late 12th century)

nominee, in defiance of Canterbury, the English king and even the Pope; not for some years after his death was the Gwynedd see brought under the sway of Canterbury. Giraldus himself put up a losing fight for the recognition of St David's as a metropolitan see.

The Norman Conquest shed its influence on monastic life too. The Celtic religious houses were not so much monastic communities as grouped hermitages within a common enclosure, belonging to no regular order, and so untouched by the reforming movements now in full swing on the continent and championed by the Normans. Within the Norman lordships these ancient monasteries were one by one attached to reformed foundations abroad and brought under regular discipline; but the new monasticism did not strike root in *pura Wallia* until the arrival of the Cistercians. The founding in 1143 of Whitland abbey in Carmarthenshire was a new landmark, for seven of the seventeen Welsh Cistercian houses set up in the course of the next generation were its offshoots. It drew extensively on the Welsh population, and provided the principal copyists and custodians of Welsh annals and Welsh poetry. The sympathies of the Cistercians, and the contemporary spread of the cult of St David (officially canonized at

turrif london'

Gryffyn'

Llywelyn the Great's son
trying to escape from Tower

Rome about 1120) as patron of all Wales, were further elements in the rise of Welsh patriotic sentiment.

Politically, Norman influence is best seen in the thirteenth century, in the career of the two Llywelyns. The first Llywelyn—Llywelyn ab Iorwerth—gained control of Gwynedd after a period of civil war between rival claimants to the inheritance of his grandfather Owain Gwynedd, and he made it his deliberate policy to turn Gwynedd into a modern state after the best feudal models of the age, with an administration of Norman pattern. How exactly it was done we cannot know, since so few of the records of independent Gwynedd have survived; but we do know that he appointed a very able seneschal, Ednyfed Fychan, whose family he endowed with extensive lands in individual proprietorship—an important step towards freeing Welsh society from what was now becoming the encumbrance of the *gwely* system. His lawyers also strove to make violent crime an offence for which the criminal must answer not just to the victim's kindred but to the prince's court.

His ultimate aim was to achieve over all Wales a feudal overlordship such as Welsh rulers since Hywel Dda had fitfully acknowledged in the kings of England. During his reign he extended Gwynedd to its ancient limits, covering the whole of North Wales except Montgomeryshire, and consolidated his position by marrying King John's daughter Joan—a base daughter, it is true, but bastardy was less of a bar in Welsh than in English law. This did not prevent him from siding with the barons who extorted Magna Carta from King John; and three clauses in the charter promised the righting of Welsh wrongs and the return of hostages. In the following year Llywelyn presided over a council of Welsh princes at Aberdovey. He was in effect master of the whole country except the modern shires of Pembroke, south Carmarthen, Glamorgan and Radnor; and wider ambitions are suggested by the marriage of his son and four of his daughters into important Norman houses.

What he failed to achieve was the transmission to his successor of an unchallenged and undivided inheritance. His death was followed once more by a disputed succession and civil war. At last his grandson, Llywelyn ap Gruffydd, made himself master of Gwynedd, and gradually recovered the lost ground till in 1267 Henry III, weakened by the baronial opposition led by Simon de Montfort and by his unsuccessful campaigns in Wales, acknowledged him by treaty as Prince of Wales. This was the climax of his power. He soon had a more formidable antagonist to face in Edward I. And even at home the concept of a united Wales, though supported by the lawyers, the bards, the Cistercians, and some other Welsh notables and churchmen, was far from generally popular.

So with this uncertain support at home, and eyed askance by Norman lordships on his eastern and southern flanks, it was a bold step for Llywelyn to jettison his grandfather's policy of feudal allegiance to the English crown. It brought on his head two full-scale invasions, in which many of his former Welsh allies and vassals deserted him. When in 1282 he was slain in a chance encounter near Builth, the cause for which he and his grandfather had fought so stoutly collapsed like a house of cards. Welsh political independence was at an end.

Further Reading

N. K. Chadwick (ed.), *Studies in Early British History*, 1954.

Id. (ed.), *Studies in the Early British Church*, 1958.

K. H. Jackson, *Language and History in Early Britain*, 1953.

J. P. Clancy, *The Earliest Welsh Poetry*, 1970.

Cyril Fox, 'The boundary line of Cymru' (*Brit. Acad. Proceedings*, xxvi), 1940.

V. E. Nash Williams, *Early Christian Inscriptions in Wales*, 1950.

E. G. Bowen, *The Settlements of the Celtic Saints in Wales*, 1954.

Gwyn Jones and Thomas Jones (trans.), *The Mabinogion*, 1949.

G. R. J. Jones, 'The tribal system in Wales' (*Welsh Hist. Rev.*, i), 1961.

J. G. Edwards, *The Principality of Wales, 1267–1967* (Caernarvonshire Hist. Soc.), 1969.

III

A Conquered People
1282–1485

Edward I's settlement of Gwynedd was harsh, but not vindictive. Those who came to terms with the new government, as most of the *uchelwyr* and the new official class hastened to do, were still eligible for office; and if the higher ranks of the bureaucracy, such as most of the sheriffs and constables of castles, were monopolized by the conquerors, the subordinate posts—those which brought their holders into closest contact with the ordinary Welsh countryman—were frequently held by members of the old families. There are also early signs of a deliberate policy of enticing ambitious young Welshmen into the royal service in London to keep them out of mischief at home.

At home the Conquest was less revolutionary in its effects than might have been expected. There were no large-scale displacements of population as in the earlier Norman conquest of Glamorgan or the later English plantations in Ireland. Fundamentally it was just an enforced change of feudal allegiance. In the recently-conquered lands west of the Conwy —the core of Gwynedd—Llywelyn's revenues and princely rights passed to the English crown. The region was administered by English officials from Caernarvon, one of Llywelyn's former seats of government. Here Edward built the most imposing of his castles, plundering the long-deserted Segontium for some of his stonework.

The castle, built in conscious imitation of the walls of imperial Constantinople, was designed to be the seat of the highly-paid justiciar (or viceroy) of North Wales at least until

Caernarvon castle and town in 1750

such time as Edward should have a son old enough to represent the crown there himself. This did not happen till in 1301 the title of Prince of Wales was revived in favour of the future Edward II, who had been born at Caernarvon and now had his official seat there. But Caernarvon saw little or nothing of him, for until he succeeded to the throne he was employed mainly in his father's Scottish campaigns, the administration of the Principality being left to officials on the spot.

So began the practice, which has continued to our own day, of conferring this historic Welsh title on the king's eldest son.

34

In the troubled days of the fifteenth century it became for a time little more than a convenient way of designating, even in babyhood, the next in succession to a frequently disputed crown, but initially it was not conferred till the heir had reached years of discretion. Those *uchelwyr* who had held their land directly from the Llywelyns, such as the descendants of the great seneschal, Ednyfed Fychan (who remained a family of consequence, with wide estates and a place in the governing hierarchy), continued to hold them of the crown as 'baronies'; to such men the acceptance of the new order must have been easier when they found they were paying their dues and services to a Prince of Wales—and one born in Wales too!

Even the administrative and legal reorganization of Llywelyn's lands left intact much that was familiar. Gwynedd west of the Conwy was carved up into the three shires of Anglesey, Caernarvon and Merioneth, with the familiar English apparatus of sheriff, shire court and the hierarchy of local officials. The sheriff was nearly always English; but the shire was simply a regrouping of older Welsh territorial divisions, which retained their importance and their local courts. Here the same sort of people met for the same sort of business as in the days before the conquest.

As for the law, the long process of erosion of immemorial custom was speeded up. Welsh criminal law finally went by the board; in civil suits the law, 'whereto the people of Wales have been long accustomed', was kept alive, and the legal profession, 'skilled in the laws of Hywel Dda', retained its importance; but the speedier and cheaper processes of English common law gradually prevailed, especially in the Principality itself, where the courts were more directly under English control. Naturally the official language was Latin or Norman French, but a Welsh lawyer would have no more difficulty in translating into official jargon what his client told him than would his English counterpart.

Whether material conditions were made harder by the financial demands of the English crown cannot be resolved without fuller knowledge of conditions under the independent princes. Certainly government was harsh, as medieval governments tended to be, and certainly the fact that many of its agents were strangers to the language and tradition of the people—apt, therefore, to be contemptuous and overbearing— did not help to sweeten relations. Local oppression was often answered by local revolt, which sometimes swelled into wider dimensions.

Edward's statute of 1284 referred primarily to the lands he had most recently conquered—the hard core of Llywelyn's dominions. Llywelyn's conquests in west Wales had been annexed earlier, and similarly reshaped into the two shires of Cardigan and Carmarthen. Gwynedd east of the Conwy and as far as the Dee was partly conferred on Norman barons who had helped the king, and partly placed under the earl of Chester, who was normally the king's eldest son. Elsewhere in Wales the Conquest had little direct effect. Powys, which had remained implacably hostile to Llywelyn, survived, much shrunken, as a dependent feudal barony under its native line. The crown and marcher lordships which covered the rest of Wales remained much as they had been before.

And so Wales, until the Tudor Act of Union, was left with no defined frontier, no central authority except what the English crown could wield through its officials or its feudal barons, no single administrative capital, no uniform system of law, no unifying principle except the Welsh language and the culture and traditions it enshrined. The country was divided into principality, royal lordships and Norman or Welsh baronial lordships; or, more compendiously, Wales and the Marches. At first the distinction was a real one. For perhaps a century after the Conquest, as long as the administration at Caernarvon and Carmarthen was working effectively and the Princes of Wales really ruled, the Principality at least had some internal unity, and the king's writ really ran there. But in the Marches, with their innumerable petty lordships, life went on as before, until 'lack of governance' culminated in the Wars of the Roses and was resolved under the Tudors by the establishment of a

Strata Florida Abbey

new unity in the Acts of Union. Long before this, however, conditions in the Principality itself had deteriorated to a point where there was little to choose between it and the Marches.

Yet through all the administrative patchwork there ran a persistent and distinctive thread of Welsh life. Welsh tenures survived, and Welsh poetry was written, in the Marches at least as much as in the Principality. The bards circulated through both, and an *uchelwr*, to all outward appearance indistinguishable from a Norman marcher lord, might retain his household bard and cultivate the traditional 'strict metres'. Dafydd ap Gwilym, generally acclaimed as Wales's premier poet, sprang from an official family in a Norman lordship. Through the bardic schools the standards of poetry were maintained and refined, and it was cherished and copied in Cistercian houses like Strata Florida.

Politically the Conquest brought to the bardic order a diminished status, and generally the bards of the next generation soft-pedalled warlike and political themes. Yet, inevitably, it was they who cultivated the sense of nostalgia, breaking out

A page from earliest known ms of Dafydd ap Gwilym, Peniarth MSS., National Library

Carreg Cennen castle, Carmarthenshire

occasionally into the well-worn apotheosis of long-dead heroes and prophecies of their glorious return to earth; more often into regrets, provoked by some specific grievance, for a vanishing social order. Well on in the fifteenth century a bard from one of the north-eastern lordships—himself, incidentally, descended from English officials—lamented the execution for murder, in pursuit of an old family feud, of a man highly skilled in music and poetry; and he expressed his hatred for the crabbed 'law of London' which had done to death a veritable nightingale for an offence which 'Hywel's law' would have expiated with a blood-fine.

The bards, however, were a highly selective group—selective in respect of both birth and skill. They did not necessarily reflect or influence the sentiments of the common man. How he felt about the Conquest we cannot know. To the peasant, whether bond or free, who went on tilling the same plot or tending the same flocks, it can hardly have been a matter of acute concern whether the lord of the land was Welsh or Anglo-Norman, unless the steward with whom he came into direct contact was conspicuously oppressive or overbearing. On the other hand, the Edwardian castles were a standing reminder to the Welsh of their conquered status. Caernarvon was only one of many; in addition to its three companions forming an iron ring around the core of Gwynedd, Edward built three more in North and two in South Wales, as well as repairing or rebuilding five castles the Welsh had originally built for their own protection. Seven were also built during the reign by lords marcher; it was indeed an age of 'castle government'.

Attached to most of the castles was a borough, sometimes walled, where Welshmen could legally acquire neither land nor burgess rights nor engage in trade—despite which a few burgesses with unimpeachable Welsh names had infiltrated into Conway within a couple of decades. The deprivation would not be acutely felt by many, but the very existence of these alien islands kept proclaiming that they were second-class citizens in their own land.

The Welsh were soon to be reminded that they were second-class churchmen too, but that lay ahead; on balance the immediate effects of the Conquest were beneficial to the Welsh Church. In all four dioceses the bishops chosen during the half-century following 1282 were men of learning and reforming zeal, and most of them had roots in their dioceses and a knowledge of the language of their countrymen; at least one of those appointed to Llandaff by Edward I, though English by birth, learned Welsh during his tenure of the see. Under this dispensation the Church recovered rapidly from the devastation caused by the Wars of Independence without losing its hold on the conquered people.

Before the middle of the fourteenth century things began to change for the worse. The administration of the first English Prince of Wales had not been unsuccessful, and when he succeeded as King Edward II he was able to build up a Welsh official class with a strong personal loyalty to himself. His murder was bitterly resented by this group. Moreover, for thirty-six years after Edward II's accession, there was no Prince of Wales, and so another focus of loyalty was removed. Edward III revived the title for the Black Prince, who in 1346 led between four and five thousand Welshmen to fight the French. Picked companies of these were clothed in their national colours of white and green—'the first troops', it has been

The Anian Pontifical, Bangor cathedral (c. 1260–1305)

41

Welsh archer   *Welsh spearman*

claimed, 'to appear on a Continental battlefield in national uniform'. These were the men who materially helped to win the battle of Crécy. In all, the stream of Welsh recruits to the French wars has been reckoned in hundreds of thousands. In Wales as in England, Crécy created a proud legend; it also provided a new outlet for the fighting instincts of the Welsh and so gave the government at home a quarter-century's respite from Welsh turbulence.

The calm was only on the surface. A grand-nephew of the last Llywelyn, known in Welsh history and legend as Owain Lawgoch and to the French as Yvain de Galles, deserted and won victories for the French which helped to turn the tide of war. So completely did he gain the confidence of his new masters that he persuaded them in 1372 to mount a full-scale expedition against England and to recognize him as the rightful Prince of Wales. He somehow contrived to contact malcontents in Gwynedd, but the expedition never got farther than Guernsey and Welsh reactions could not be put to the test.

As the fourteenth century wore on, it brought with it mounting causes of discontent, not all of them peculiar to Wales. The French campaigns were expensive, and Edward III — misled, perhaps, by the relative quiescence of Wales — showed none of his father's or his grandfather's wariness about Welsh susceptibilities. Wales became a milch cow from which an endless stream of men and money could be squeezed. Administration worsened, and the Church in particular suffered. Not only was the financial screw tightened, but from about 1340 there was an increasing propensity to use bishoprics and the better-paid posts in cathedrals and parishes as a dumping ground for household officials, till Welsh-speaking clerics were edged out of all the upper grades of the hierarchy.

The only check on this tendency was the occasional intervention of the papacy, to implement the principle laid down in the preceding century that provision should be made, 'where there are people of divers tongues', to ensure the celebration of divine service 'according to diversities of rite and language'. But papal interventions became rarer as the papacy was weakened by schism and less able to withstand the claims of secular monarchs. The result was a fissure between the upper and the lower clergy, who thus swelled the discontented elements in the community and showed a tendency to take the lead in local risings.

Deeper still were the economic causes of discontent. Following a series of bad harvests, the 'Black Death' in 1348–9 devastated Western Europe, and the social order was undermined. Hit by heavy taxation, the lords of the land sought to exact money dues in place of the traditional services from their tenants. In bond communities these dues were levied collectively. It was on these huddled masses, living at a bare subsistence level, that the plague fell heaviest, yet attempts were made to squeeze the full quota from the survivors. The bondsmen shrank in numbers to less than a tenth of the population; even the freemen had often to dispose of their cattle to meet demands for cash they did not possess. Sometimes there were wholesale flights from the countryside, and, as so often happens in such crises, the enterprising and ruthless were able to exploit the situation.

It must have been a time of widespread misery, yet, although the fourteenth century was one of the great ages of Welsh poetry, little of this social distress and political unrest is reflected in the verse. The official bards were aristocrats, concerned in the main with perfecting their art and experimenting in new verse forms. A solitary poem, full of rich imagery, in praise of the ploughman, refers vaguely to his sufferings but is in the main an encomium of the simple life, close to nature and remote from war and politics. But popular verse, which would bring us closer to the lives of the masses, circulated in the main orally, and little of it has come down to us. The poems were generally sung to the accompaniment of harp or *crwth*,

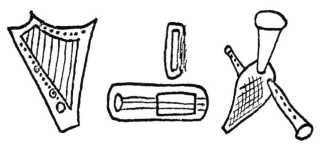

Welsh musical instruments

horn or bagpipe, but although in bardic schools and eisteddfodau music took its place with poetry, no written Welsh music of the period can be identified with any confidence; but surviving indications in later music suggest that it was as advanced and sophisticated as the poetry it accompanied.

Of the general misery of the masses the most convincing evidence is the national revolt that broke out at the very end of the century. In England the Black Death was followed within a generation by the Peasants' Revolt; in Wales it took more like half a century for the smouldering discontent to explode. What laid the train was the deposition of the Black Prince's son, Richard II, who had a substantial following among the Welsh. What sparked it off was a boundary dispute between two lords marcher—commonplace save in one important detail. One of the contestants ruled in a north-eastern lordship created by Edward I; the other, though educated in England and experienced in warfare under the English crown, was very conscious of the blood of the princes of Powys and Deheubarth in his veins. He was Owain ap Gruffydd, lord of Glyndyfrdwy, known more briefly to the Welsh as Owain Glyn Dŵr, to Shakespeare as Glendower. The English were con-

44

vinced he could 'call spirits from the vasty deep', but this may
have been due to his capacity, as guerilla leader, for materializ-
ing from nowhere, or to the supposed incantations of his
companion bards, who appeared to English eyes as reincarna-
tions of the Druids.

Owain styled himself Prince of Wales (a title Richard II's
supplanter Henry IV had already bestowed on 'Prince Hal'),
and in that capacity equipped himself with a great seal, a
singularly able clerical chancellor, and all the paraphernalia
of government; he also summoned two 'parliaments', more
widely representative than those of the Llywelyns, and made
his authority felt over almost the whole of Wales except
Pembrokeshire and some of the castles. By savage racial laws
against the Welsh, the English king had helped to exacerbate
feeling, and Glyn Dŵr secured a valuable pawn when he
captured Edmund Mortimer, whose line stood in legitimate
succession to the throne, and married him to his daughter.
This brought into his camp Mortimer's brother-in-law 'Harry
Hotspur', justiciar of North Wales—for both had grievances
against the English king. There followed the wildcat scheme
for a partition of south Britain between Glyn Dŵr and his new
allies, which would have extended the frontier of Wales far
east into England.

Abroad, the self-styled Prince of Wales entered into dealings
with Henry IV's other
enemies. The Irish proved
unresponsive, but the
Scots were ready to recognize him. With the French
he concluded a treaty
under which the invasion
projected thirty years
earlier became a reality.
To cement the alliance he
negotiated in 1406 with
the anti-pope at Avignon
(who was recognized by
France and Scotland while
England clung to Rome),

Arms of Glyn Dŵr as Prince of Wales

offering to transfer to him the allegiance of Wales on the establishment of an independent archbishopric (confined to Welshmen) at St David's, and of two Welsh universities. By this time, however, Owain's power was waning. He never had much joy of his allies, English or foreign, and now home support was falling away, as his followers submitted to the offer of free pardon. Owain himself spurned all such overtures and continued his guerilla activities long after he was able to put an army into the field. Exactly when and how he died no one knows. His son accepted the offer the father had declined, and took service in the English court, in company with one of his kinsmen from the house of Ednyfed, known to history as Owain Tudor, the grandfather of Henry VII.

Releasing the rebels from the penalties of treason did not, of course, mean releasing the Welsh people from the oppressive racial laws, and devastation and dislocation caused by the war — not least in the Church — only intensified the miseries of the preceding century. Yet although the rising had failed to achieve its object and had left a long trail of misery behind it, it bred in the Welsh a new and exhilarating self-confidence. Despite the many who hung back from his cause, or actively opposed or deserted it, Glyn Dŵr had gone further towards uniting all the ancient divisions of Wales than even the Llywelyns. Powys had always resisted them; Glyn Dŵr was himself a man of Powys. In addition he had given Wales a new standing on the continent, with France as an ally and French spokesmen explaining to the doctors at the Council of Constance (which met in 1414 in an effort to heal the schism in the papacy) that Wales was no part of the English 'nation'.

Glyn Dŵr had never been finally defeated in the field. He had just faded away; maybe he would reappear, or if not he, one of those other Deliverers the bards were forever promising. There was no despairing elegy on Glyn Dŵr, as there had been on Llywelyn. Indeed little of the poetic output of the age is in a minor key, unless it be the work of the outstanding religious poet Siôn Cent. And whatever may have been the condition of the depressed classes, at least there was no major pestilence on the scale of the Black Death. The renewal of the war with France bred new heroic sagas; for although, as Prince of Wales,

46

Abergavenny church, Sir William ap Thomas tomb

the new king had taken the field against Glyn Dŵr while the French were his allies, *uchelwyr* from every corner of Wales sought adventure under the English banner. Many returned loaded with knighthoods and booty, ready to assume leadership at home; for them the penal laws of the Glyn Dŵr epoch were allowed to fall into oblivion.

This period saw the rise of the new Welsh 'gentry' class which continued to rule the country, often through the same families, till the nineteenth century. Many of them rose to position and wealth by serving the English crown, even against their own rebellious countrymen; yet this was no obstacle to their remaining jealous guardians of the language and its literature. The new gentry dug themselves in (once the native system of landholding had begun to give way to consolidated estates and farms) through profits from military service or civil office, or the acquisition of crown lands, vacant 'bond' holdings, or other lands 'escheated' to the crown as a result of treason or failure of heirs.

An example of the first is provided by the Herbert family, Norman in origin but Welsh in sentiment through intermarriage, who were brought into prominence by the military

47

Dynevor castle

prowess of the Agincourt knight Sir William ap Thomas, and
reaped a rich harvest in lands and prestige throughout Wales.
Of those who careers were based on civic office, the house of
Dynevor in west Wales provides a good example. In the early
fifteenth century Gruffydd ap Nicolas took a lease of the crown
lordship of Dynevor, and entered into the service of that great
Renaissance prince Humphrey, duke of Gloucester, justice of
both North and South Wales. As the duke's deputy in the
western shires he was able to hold an eisteddfod comparable
with that held by the Lord Rhys nearly three centuries earlier.
The family has retained its local importance; Gruffydd's
collateral descendant Lord Dynevor was one of the Welsh
peers supporting the Prince of Wales at his investiture in 1969.

In North Wales Gwilym ap Gruffydd, who founded the fortunes of the family of Griffith of Penrhyn, rose to eminence
through timely desertion of Glyn Dŵr, and was thus able to
lord it in what may have been the first house in North Wales
to be built on a scale approaching that of the princely *llysoedd*.
His descendants were to monopolize the chief public office in
the Principality in late medieval and early Tudor days.

The occupation of escheat lands or vacant holdings did not

become a vital factor until after the Wars of the Roses had wrought further havoc in the social order, but the nuclei of what were to become important estates, like that of the Cheshire Bulkeleys who so long dominated Anglesey and Caernarvonshire, were to be seen even before that. Often enough it was from the boroughs that this process began, since the burgesses were supplied by trade with the necessary cash.

The rise of the gentry had its reflection in domestic architecture. This is the period when the bards begin to embroider their tributes to their patrons with praise of their houses. It is true that these descriptive passages tend to conform to a pattern, deriving from the specifications for the prince's house set out in the laws. It is also true that the bard is apt to be more interested in the good cheer provided than in the house itself. None the less, bardic descriptions often supplement what can be learned about the medieval Welsh house from the scant and battered survivals.

Merchant's house at Tenby, 15th century

The hall at Sycharth in Denbighshire, where Glyn Dŵr lived in his prosperous and peaceful days, was sacked to such purpose that archaeology unaided can do little towards an intelligible reconstruction. The Herbert mansion of Coldbrook, near Abergavenny, lasted, with much later rebuilding, from the thirteenth or fourteenth century until

Tretower court, Breconshire, east front (14th–15th century)

it was pulled down some fifteen years ago—in such haste as to preclude detailed examination. Apart from bardic panegyrics, all we know of medieval Penrhyn is what lies buried in the cellars of the pseudo-Norman castle superimposed on it in the last century.

These, of course, were the houses of a very limited class, for the most part newly enriched. But, as in all other ages, new fashions in building soon spread to the medium-sized dwelling houses of a widening circle of gentry and then yeomen. The rehousing of the peasantry, who could not afford to employ masons and carpenters, came very much later; until the eighteenth century they had to be content with the more perishable structures they could erect themselves. The 'long house', with entrance at the narrow end rather than the long front (and often through kitchen or byre) is in the main a peculiarity of west Wales and the south-west, but its age and purpose are in dispute. Farm buildings, whether connecting with the main living-quarters or not, are inevitably a feature of domestic architecture in a country where most of the gentry farmed their own lands.

The Wars of the Roses helped to consolidate the leadership

Harlech castle, Merioneth

of the rising gentry. On the one hand they brought in their wake a generation of social chaos, when deadly feuds flourished and areas of wild woodland became haunts of outlaws. On the other hand they also brought a new accession of lands and honours to Welsh leaders. The house of York, which drew much of its strength from the Marches, embodied the claims of the Mortimers, Glyn Dŵr's old allies, and Edward IV stood in direct descent from the daughter of Llywelyn the Great. Lancaster, as long as it held the crown, held also the extensive crown lands of the Principality and so had widespread support there, though some of this naturally faded away when York became the ruling dynasty. The stoutest Welsh champions of York were the Herberts, who became the most powerful family in Wales under Edward IV. But Owain Tudor's marriage to Henry V's widow, and that of his son Edmund Tudor to the eventual heiress of Lancaster, threw the powerful influence of this family on to the Lancastrian side.

Yet these divisions were far from destroying the sense of national pride to which the Glyn Dŵr revolt, the popular acceptance of the myths of Geoffrey of Monmouth and the

51

bardic prophesies had all contributed. The bards provided a bond of union underlying all the divisions, for they found a welcome in the halls of both factions, and they fostered pride in the prowess of Welsh leaders in both armies. The gallantry of the Welsh garrison at Harlech, almost the last in the land to submit to Edward IV, became an epic cherished in national tradition. Yet the eventual capture of the castle by the Herbert brothers further increased their Welsh renown; and Guto'r Glyn, a Yorkist bard from the north-eastern Marches, urged them not to revenge themselves on the men of Gwynedd, but to use their prestige to unite the Welsh in one more bid for the hegemony of Britain.

This striking poem reveals the wider outlook on the Wars of the Roses of those Welshmen who were not moved solely by love of adventure, plunder or power. Their aim was much the same as that of their forefathers in the days of Magna Carta or of Simon de Montfort: to snatch what could be gained for Wales out of English divisions and distractions. But the issue was now no longer one of mere Welsh autonomy under English suzerainty, as with the Llywelyns. Geoffrey of Monmouth had reminded them that, as a Welsh Catholic exile put it to a Scots co-religionist and fellow-exile a couple of centuries later, 'We are the old and true inhabiters and owners of the isle of Brittany: these others be but usurpers and mere possessors.' The 'nationalism' fostered by the Glyn Dŵr movement might more aptly be dubbed imperialism. The leader himself contemplated annexing to Wales most of Cheshire, Shropshire and Herefordshire—a substantial Cambria Irredenta with a predominantly English population.

In bardic panegyrics the hallmark of 'Welshness' is always the language; but the more exalted patriots were now dreaming of a Britain where Welsh was again the dominant tongue and Welshmen the key men in government. An Elizabethan manuscript purporting to describe life in the Wales of her day gives a clue to the way in which such poems, with their easily-memorized, alliterative passages, could reach vast audiences. It tells of assemblies on the hillside on holidays at which 'theire harpers and crowthers singe them songes of the doings of theire auncestors . . . and . . . the intended prophetts and saincts of that cuntrie'. And this was obviously a survival of long-cherished custom.

In the concluding phases of the Wars of the Roses the fulfilment of some of these prophetic utterances seemed at hand. So long as Edward IV was on the throne, Wales remained quiet. He had promoted Welsh supporters like the Herberts, and had dealt leniently with those who had opposed him; a few years later he sent the infant Prince of Wales with a council to Ludlow to stimulate loyalty. But Welsh support for the house of York faded away after his death. When the Prince succeeded to the throne, at thirteen, as Edward V, he was promptly deposed and cast into the Tower by his uncle and official Protector, who had himself proclaimed king as Richard III.

Whether or not, as soon came to be believed, the 'wicked uncle' was the murderer of the boy king and his younger brother, he got no backing in Wales. The Herbert brothers were dead, and in 1471, the main Lancastrian line came to an end with the death in prison of Henry VI and that of his son on the battlefield. There now remained only the Beaufort branch, represented by Margaret, widow of Owain Tudor's son Edmund, whom his half-brother Henry VI had made earl of Richmond. Margaret never claimed the throne for herself, but bent her efforts towards promoting the claims of her son Henry, heir to his dead father's earldom.

Gradually all eyes in Wales turned to Henry Tudor as the mab darogan (or son of prophecy). Rhys ap Thomas, grandson of the founder of the fortunes of Dynevor, after coming to terms with the house of York, deserted it for the Tudor claimant, bringing with him a wealth of military experience; other gentlemen of good family from up and down Wales, seasoned in the French wars and experienced in

Henry VII, bust by Torrigiano

Mostyn Christ, Bangor cathedral

civil office, were ready to place their arms at his disposal. But the backbone of the movement was Edmund Tudor's brother Jasper, a consistent and devoted Lancastrian. It was he who was chiefly responsible for the upbringing of his nephew Henry until they had to flee from Wales to Brittany. Here Jasper laid plans for the young earl's bid for the crown and for reconciling old Yorkists by marrying him to Edward IV's daughter Elizabeth.

We can probably trace his hand, too, in the growing boldness with which the swelling chorus of prophetic verse, exalting the imperial destiny of the Welsh, came to be linked with the Tudor claim. But quite apart from this, there appears, during the latter half of the fifteenth century, a lifting of the spirits of the Welsh, at a time when the long-drawn wars, intrigues and political murders were reducing England to a state of weary indifference. It is seen not only in poetry, but in the great spate of church building and adornment to repair the devastation of the Glyn Dŵr period. It was financed partly by the bounty of the rich, partly by the offerings of the numerous pilgrims to popular shrines. Many churches were rebuilt after the fashionable 'perpendicular' style; others had a second aisle added, often to accommodate a chapel to the Virgin, whose cult was particularly widespread in the Wales of this period. Many were enriched with delicately-carved rood screens of native workmanship; some with wall paintings or carvings in stone.

To some extent, of course, these advances may be attributed to the rising wealth of the new gentry, and to increasing commercial activity, especially in the southern ports. Whether they betokened a greater vigour in spiritual life may be doubted; at least monastic numbers were in decline, and even the Cistercians were tending to abandon manual activities and to lease out their sheep runs to laymen. But the high-pitched expectations aroused by the belief that the long-promised Deliverer was really at hand cannot be discounted.

Further Reading

A. J. Taylor, 'The King's Works in North Wales', in H. M. Colvin (ed.), *History of the King's Works*, i, 1963.

W. Rees, *South Wales and the March, 1284–1485: a Social and Agrarian Study*, 1924.

Glanmor Williams, *The Welsh Church from Conquest to Reformation*, 1962.

D. L. Evans, 'Some notes on the history of the principality of Wales in the time of the Black Prince', *Transactions of Hon. Soc. of Cymmrodorion*, 1925–6.

W. Rees, 'The Black Death in Wales', *Transactions of Royal Historical Society*, 1920.

Glanmor Williams, *Owen Glendower* (Clarendon Biographies), 1965.

H. T. Evans, *Wales and the Wars of the Roses*, 1915.

IV

Union, Reformation and Renaissance, 1485–1630

On landing at Milford Haven, Henry Tudor sent out letters to the principal gentry of Wales declaring 'the great confidence that we have to the nobles and commons of this our principalitye', and promising to restore 'the people of the same to their erst libertyes, deliveringe them of such miserable servitudes as they have pyteously longe stand in'. It was a shrewd gesture, and it brought good dividends—even if the recipients may not always have put the same construction on the 'erst liberties' as their would-be deliverer. The 'miserable servitudes' were easier to interpret: the primary reference was obviously to the laws under which Welshmen were deprived of the normal rights of citizenship by the mere fact of their Welsh blood, irrespective of their allegiance. These laws had undergone considerable erosion during the Wars of the Roses, but Henry speeded up the process—first by granting individual letters of denizenship admitting prominent Welsh supporters to the full benefits of the common law, then by charters making the same concessions collectively to his Principality and to some of the marcher lordships that had fallen into his hands. This was generally acceptable—except to the English burgesses of the chartered boroughs, who naturally resented the admission of 'natives' to their special privileges. They put up a tough resistance, and the matter was still unsettled when Henry died.

Whether Henry intended anything more than the removal of these relatively recent 'servitudes' is open to doubt. Certainly some of those who flocked to his banner expected more, but not all of them wanted the same 'liberties'. As so often, there was a clash between the interests of the richer and more influential freeholders and those of their humbler neighbours, to say nothing of the bondsmen. Among the *uchelwyr* there was no desire to return to the 'laws of Hywel Dda', with their rigid rule of equal inheritance among the members of the *gwely*, and the formidable obstacles they presented to the acquisition of land outside it.

We have seen how the Llywelyns themselves drilled great holes in the traditional system in the interests of their own 'official' class. This had caused murmuring among their subjects, but since then the benefits of the English system of primogeniture, and the growing freedom in the transfer of land under English law, had undeceived the more ambitious and enterprising on the blessings of the old Welsh order. For years Welsh lawyers had been devising ingenious means of getting round these ancient restraints; and it is suggestive that when, later on, Welsh representatives were admitted to Parliament, the first issue on which they took collective action was a bill extending to the Welsh landowner English methods of conveyancing.

The question of the bond tenants was a thornier one. The great reduction in their numbers following 1348 had dealt a heavy blow at the royal revenues. Attempts to re-people the waste places had not been successful, and recourse was often had to the issue of licences to freeholders to acquire vacant bond holdings, or to legalize encroachments already made; for example, the settlement in derelict Nantconwy of the Wynns of Gwydir. But there were still burdensome incidents attached to bond tenure, which the new occupants tried to shrug off. Great landlords with bondsmen of their own, however, were no less disturbed than the crown at the prospect of losing this source of revenue. What Henry eventually did was to grant to his bond tenants 'a general emancipation and liberty'. This emancipation, of course, meant the conferring of a new liberty, not the revival of an ancient one, and naturally none of these concessions was made without a substantial money recompense.

Political liberties were another matter again. There were expectations that, with a Welsh king on the throne, the

Carew castle, entrance to Sir Rhys ap Thomas's Hall

administration of Wales, if not of England, would fall into the hands of his compatriots. Only to a limited extent were these expectations fulfilled. In the Church, it is true, Henry broke with the practice of filling Welsh sees with partisans from England or abroad; three of Henry's appointments to St

Asaph, two to St David's and possibly one to Bangor, were of native-born Welshmen. In civil administration his uncle, Jasper Tudor, was his right-hand man in England and also chief justiciar of Wales. Of the other Welsh notables who had risen to prominence under the Yorkist kings, Sir Rhys ap Thomas, who by bringing Welsh forces to his aid had helped to decide the day at Bosworth, held almost regal sway in south-west Wales. The male line of the Herberts came to an end soon after Henry's accession, but in the next reign the earldom was revived and the old ascendancy resumed in another branch.

Four years after his accession Henry revived the dormant title of Prince of Wales for his son, whom he had named Arthur as a tribute to Welsh sentiment. Several important border lordships were also conferred on Arthur, and at the age of fifteen he was sent with a body of counsellors to Ludlow to exercise his dual authority. Henry cautiously chose as members of the prince's council experienced Yorkist bureaucrats rather than Welsh magnates whose feuds might nullify his efforts.

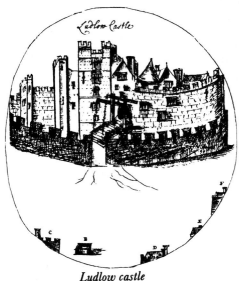

Ludlow castle

This council became a focal point for the Welsh gentry, giving the land a sort of extra-territorial capital at Ludlow

Ludlow castle, Prince Arthur's chapel

and a link with the central government. From the death of
Prince Arthur it carried on under its own president without
the visible presence of royalty, except during the few years
when Henry VIII sent his daughter Mary (then heir apparent
to the throne) to Ludlow with the title Governor of Wales.
Following Yorkist practice, the presidents were generally border bishops; and not till mid-century did these begin to be
replaced by men with strong territorial influence in Wales
itself—notably the two earls of Pembroke and Sir Henry Sidney,
whose presidencies covered most of the second half of the
century.

A bardic ode to the victor of Bosworth hailed him as 'emperor'. Henry's own ambitions were more modest. Indeed he
was too busy establishing his throne to formulate any coherent
policy for Wales. The bardic apocalypse had to wait. But if his
Welsh compatriots were still far from attaining the promised
lordship in Wales itself—still less in all Britain—many of them
were comfortably ensconced in the royal bodyguard or in other
places of profit around the king's person in London, and
English ears were becoming attuned to the unaccustomed
sound of Welsh spoken at the royal court itself.

As Prince of Wales, Henry VIII never visited his Principality.
Nearly twenty years after his accession he was assured that

'the generalitie of the poer people ther do apply themselfe diligently in hosbandry labores, tyllage and plowynge more then hath byn sithe the tyme of eny man's memory levyng', and that 'ther be not soo many universalle misdoers and offenders as in tyme passed'. The report was premature: soon afterwards west Wales was in turmoil because Sir Rhys ap Thomas's grandson, the popular Rhys ap Gruffydd, had been passed over for the post of chamberlain of South Wales in favour of an English lord marcher—the grandfather of Elizabeth's Essex. The quarrel was patched up, but the ambitions of the house of Dynevor remained a festering sore, and two years later the king—by now in the throes of his quarrel with Rome—had Rhys executed rather than risk a Welsh uprising under a popular leader. It meant the replacement of the powerful Dynevor interest in the south-west by that of the Devereux—who were in turn to prove a thorn in the side of some of Henry's successors.

Feuds between Welsh *uchelwyr* and English bureaucrats, between Principality and Marches, were in danger of becoming endemic when Thomas Cromwell rose to power. He was a tidy-minded administrator, and what could be more untidy than the tangle of jurisdictions which Wales and the Marches presented? Cromwell had connections with Wales through his son-in-law, but his first impulse was to restore order by bringing back some of the 'miserable servitudes' from which Henry VII had freed the Welsh. Advice on Welsh affairs was given to him by the new president, Roland Lee—another bishop, who was far from 'affable to any of the walshrie': he boasted of five thousand executions in six years, and did not disdain to ride after malefactors in person.

Cromwell, however, was soon disabused of this purely negative policy, and his was the hand behind the appearance in 1536 of the most comprehensive code for the whole area that had been framed since Edward I's Statute of Wales. It was indeed more comprehensive than Edward's statute, since it tackled what he had evaded—the problem of the Marches—and tackled it once for all by abolishing them outright. The eastern rim was tacked on to the neighbouring English shires; the rest was carved into five new shires, administered on the familiar pattern and added to the Principality of Wales, which for the first time was given a definite administrative boundary.

This Act, and the supplementary Act added seven years later, are commonly known as the Welsh Acts of Union. Their most important effect, it has been pointed out, was to 'unify Wales politically within itself'. Henceforth the country was under uniform law. Welsh law and custom ceased to have legal force unless specially sanctioned by the king, although they long continued to influence social practice. English common law prevailed everywhere, but in the framing of new statute law the Welsh shires and boroughs were given their share through the extension to them, for the first time since Edward II's reign, of the English system of representation; the shires had a single member apiece and in most of them the boroughs were grouped to elect a member collectively. By the time of Elizabeth the Welsh members had learned their job and were taking an active part in proceedings. To administer the law, Wales was divided into four circuits in each of which judges went on tour twice a year to deal with major offences; these Great Sessions of Wales retained their separate existence till 1830. More important to the ordinary Welshman was the appointment in each shire of justices of the peace, chosen from among the chief local gentry to deal with minor offences and to be generally responsible for county administration. At the top of the pyramid, the Council of Wales was put on a definite statutory basis.

Formal proceedings in these courts were in English, which imposed the same sort of disability on monoglot Welsh litigants as English litigants had suffered a couple of centuries earlier when Norman French was the language of the law; but we have it on the word of a judge of Great Sessions that 'In Wales the witnesses speak Welsh, and English witnesses are interpreted in Welsh when it is required'. In the more Welsh-speaking shires the Council of Wales sometimes insisted that the justices should translate and publish its orders in Welsh, and surviving copies show that the monoglot Welshman was not left in ignorance of the law. Unfortunately, while the Act laid down that higher officials must 'use and exercise the English speech', a proposal that one at least of the judges

Wrexham church (completed under Henry VII)

should understand Welsh never bore fruit. In the lower courts, however, and among the lower officials, the use of Welsh must have been general.

It appears that, under the Acts of Union, there was in Wales wider participation in government, both locally and centrally, than there had been since the days of independence. Roland Lee protested vigorously against the perils of giving so much power to the 'walshrie'; but Thomas Crómwell, bent on carrying to a successful issue the king's breach with Rome, knew too well how easy a back door Wales could present to a foreign invader bent on restoring papal authority in the king-dom, and he therefore took the risk of associating the Welsh gentry as a whole, and not merely the few notables, with the work of government.

In the event the risk was justified, for in Wales the early stages of the religious revolution were carried through with the minimum of friction. This was not due, as has been suggested, solely to religious indifference or to greed for church lands.

63

Tintern Abbey as seen by Turner

The late fifteenth century, in fact, had been marked by a good deal of zeal in church building, and what popular Welsh verse of the period has survived betrays a lively interest in religious themes. The widespread survival of contemporary manuscript copies in Welsh of the office of the Blessed Virgin throws another sidelight on popular religion. Of heresy there is little evidence apart from some vestiges of Lollardry in the southern borderland and a few reports, at the beginning of Henry VII's reign, of heretical conversations in Pembrokeshire seaports.

More common were attacks on the avarice of the clergy and of the papal court and its agents—as for example when the town of Carmarthen protested in 1474 about a pedlar of indulgences there. So far as is known, Henry's assumption of the headship evoked no significant protest, any more than Glyn Dŵr's proposed transfer of allegiance from Pope to anti-Pope. Consequently there was no wholesale change in clerical personnel, high or low, to bring home to the man in the street the significance of what was happening.

More far-reaching in their effects on Welsh life were the dissolution of the monasteries and the plundering of the churches—the former affecting the social order, the latter touching ingrained habits of devotion. The monastic orders had long ceased to attract men in sufficient numbers to ensure the effective observance of the religious life, or even the management of their estates. The monks were far from unpopular; many houses had been warm patrons of Welsh literature and champions of the national cause, and the bards in turn paid homage to them—but with the accent on their lavish hospitality rather than their religious devotion. But when the highest number of monks in any of the Welsh houses was thirteen, it is not surprising that covetous eyes were cast on their extensive estates.

By the time of Elizabeth most of the monastic estates had passed into the hands of the Welsh gentry, and parts of the houses, or at least their furnishings, had gone to enlarge and adorn their dwellings. This did not necessarily imply acceptance of the new religious order; on the contrary many of the families which remained loyal to Rome till well on in the following century had invested liberally in monastic spoils. With the monastic estates the purchasers also acquired parochial tithe where it had been in monastic hands. This helped to tighten the control of the gentry over the Church.

The spoliation of churches began near the end of Henry VIII's reign and reached its climax under Edward VI; and there are passages in Welsh verse of the period which convey the sense of desolation at the loss of so many familiar and hallowed aids to worship. Whether the new English service books of Edward VI's reign were actually used in Welsh parishes is not known; they would have conveyed less to a monoglot congregation than the familiar Latin. Perhaps the only aspect of the Edwardian Reformation that was widely welcomed was the relaxation of the rule of clerical celibacy, which had been no part of ancient Celtic usage. The persecutions of Mary's reign claimed a few Welsh victims, but more important for the future was the little knot of Welsh scholars who had imbibed heterodox views at Oxford during the intellectual ferment that followed Luther's revolt. Two of them were churchmen who fled to the continent when Mary succeeded Edward VI; a third, the learned squire William Salesbury, buried himself in his remote Denbighshire home, immersed in works of scholarship and translation.

It was to men from this limited circle that Elizabeth turned when at the outset of her reign she was faced with three vacancies out of the four Welsh sees. For only one of the Welsh bishops took the oath to the new queen—those appointed under Mary had either been deprived or fled abroad without awaiting their fate. Their successors actively promoted the Elizabethan church order in their dioceses. All were sprung from local families. This had its seamier side: Archbishop Parker was warned (not without reason) that the Welsh 'banded so much together in kindred that the bishop could not do as he would for his alliance sake'.

The chief accession of strength to the Protestant establishment, however, came from the translation into Welsh of the Bible and Prayer Book. An Act rushed through Parliament in 1562 laid down that this work was to be completed within four years, after which the Welsh version must be adopted in all parishes 'where the Welsh tongue is commonly used'; compulsory Welsh in church to balance compulsory English in the courts! It needed an amending Act in 1863 to legalize English services for an English-speaking minority in a predominantly

Gwybrnant, birthplace of Bp. Morgan, translator of Bible

Welsh area. Until the new translation was ready, the Gospel and Epistle for the day, the Commandments, Paternoster, Creed and Litany were to be recited in Welsh.

The Welsh New Testament duly appeared in 1567. The lion's share of the work had fallen on Salesbury, but he had an able collaborator in Richard Davies, one of Elizabeth's new bishops. Davies commended the work in an 'Epistle to the Welsh' embodying the patriotic myth, long current in border Lollard circles, that the Celtic Church alone had preserved the Christian faith in its original purity and embodied it in an extensive but long-vanished vernacular literature. The Reformation could thus be presented as a return to a proud Welsh past instead of an imported novelty.

Twenty-one years later the Old Testament was added, and the whole work revised, by a Denbighshire vicar and future bishop, William Morgan, who had come down from Cambridge with a high reputation as a Hebrew scholar. The translation of the Bible was for Wales the most important event of the reign, if not of the century. It set up a standard of Welsh prose writing which, unlike the classical bardic poetry, was intelligible to the masses, and so saved the language from degenerating into a rustic *patois*. But it also saved Elizabeth's government from the peril of another Ireland, with national sentiment inflamed against the intrusion of an alien religion. It was in fact the highlight of the Reformation in Wales.

With services conducted in Welsh, and no alternative form of worship available to most of the people, the new religious order slowly won its way. Penalties for non-attendance at church were at first light, and the greater gentry, especially those whose estates lay on the main highways, generally set an example of compliance. It was among the up-country squires and in ancient centres of pilgrimage that dissidence was rife. Abroad there was the group of Catholic refugees who had fled on Elizabeth's accession, including several deprived churchmen, a few scholars bent on by-passing the Protestant universities at home by completing their education abroad, and some laymen who had been drawn into political plots. They mostly congregated in the Netherlands and Italy, often flitting between the two.

At first they concentrated their efforts on smuggling into Wales Catholic literature which they translated and printed abroad; their publications included the earliest printed Welsh grammar, designed as an aid to the campaign. It was largely through their efforts that seminaries were established in connection with the new university at Douai and the English college at Rome. Nearly a hundred Welsh youths resorted to these educational centres during the reign; many of them devoted themselves after their training to the perilous task of re-converting their countrymen by personal evangelism. For by the time the first students had passed through Douai, the Pope had excommunicated Elizabeth, and (in the words of a Welsh convert), 'matters came to be more discerned and distinguished concerning religion'. Some of the new army of missionary priests landed at obscure creeks on the Welsh coast, found shelter with sympathizers, and won back for their faith waverers, or the wives and children of those whose husbands or fathers had conformed.

There was also a less peaceful side to the work of the *émigrés*. Some of them urged an invasion in the interests of Mary, Queen of Scots, which they believed could be successfully launched on the Welsh coast with strong local support. After the excommunication, invasion scares and rumours of plots abounded. None of them materialized, but the backwash reached the remotest parts of Wales. Seven years later, Whitgift began his harsh rule as vice-president of the Council of Wales, in the absence in Ireland of the milder president, Sir Henry Sidney. The drive against recusants and priests was further intensified under the presidency of Pembroke, and the country became inured to nocturnal raids, mutual denunciation among neighbours and interrogation under torture, with spies and informers round every corner, and peaceful evangelism often confused with armed treason.

A group of recusants, with several priests, had lived and worshipped for months in a cave in the Little Orme in Caernarvonshire, under the protection of an influential neighbouring family. From there they issued a Welsh translation of a work of Catholic devotion. It bore a sham continental imprint, but was almost certainly the first book to be printed in Wales. When the cave was raided in 1586 the type was found scattered and the occupants had fled; but six years later one of them— Father William Davies—was caught at Holyhead in the act of escorting some young aspirants to the priesthood to Ireland *en route* for a Spanish seminary. In the following year he suffered a traitor's death at Beaumaris. He was not the first Welsh Catholic martyr, for Richard Gwyn, a layman who had been teaching in several schools in the Wrexham area, was rash enough to ridicule in verse the new Protestant order, to consort with the missionary priests and to attempt to undermine the new-born Protestantism of some of the leading gentry of the neighbourhood. After eight trials he suffered the same barbarous death at Wrexham in 1584. He was among the forty martyrs canonized in 1970.

As a rule, no political activity was brought home to these victims. The plotting was all done abroad, and the hope of the refugees that their countrymen at home might be roused to active resistance proved a delusion. The working government of Wales was now in the hands of the gentry, and they on the whole remained more loyal to their native dynasty than to their ancestral faith. Theological convictions apart, the fact that the plotters looked to Ireland and Spain for succour, and that Wales lay directly in the path of an invasion from either quarter, told heavily against them. The smaller squires and yeomen, less accessible to currents of opinion from outside, lacked the means to provide leadership. The peasant masses proved, as always, hard to wean from deeply-ingrained religious practices; but the use in church of their familiar tongue helped to wear down prejudice, and except where the appeal of missionary priests had succeeded, they followed their traditional leaders.

Of the more advanced Protestantism which developed into Puritanism there was little sign in Wales. John Penry, one of the early Puritan martyrs, was a Breconshire man, but he left little impression on his native county. Trade brought in a small Puritan strain to some of the market towns and seaports of the south, and at Wrexham a similar element is to be found among the persecutors of Richard Gwyn. But by the end of the century the only threat to the Elizabethan church settlement came from the diminishing pockets of Catholic recusancy.

For all the turmoil of the Reformation, by the end of the century there had been a general increase in prosperity and in what contemporaries called 'civilitie'. 'A better country to govern Europe holdeth not,' was Sir Henry Sidney's comment on his experience as president. The Shrewsbury scribbler Thomas Churchyard, in an ecstatic medley of verse and prose which he dedicated to Queen Elizabeth under the title *The Worthines of Wales*, declared that

> *Ye may come there, beare purse of gold in hand,*
> *Or mightie bagges, of silver stuffed throwe,*
> *And no one man dare touch your treasure now.*

Legal records, unhappily, tell a different tale. Communal life was still punctuated by robberies and murderous affrays, and if the great men of the land no longer fought it out on the battlefield, many 'maintained' gangs of dependants to pursue family feuds on the public highway or at fairs and markets— with impunity if the patron were powerful enough. Roland Lee's gloomy predictions about misuse of public office by the turbulent Welsh gentry often appeared justified. Indeed, if one believed half the accusations they flung against each other in Star Chamber or Great Sessions one would be left wondering how everyday life in Wales survived at all. But the history of a country does not lie in its legal records, and other sources present a picture of expanding trade, growing population and increasing prosperity, with these same turbulent gentry participating effectively in the humdrum tasks of government—to the enrichment of their political education.

The chief gainers from a more orderly society were those who had risen to the top during the preceding age, and were all set to take advantage of the opportunities afforded by a more fluid land market, and by the wider openings for profitable matches in England which came with the assimilation of

Myddelton brass, Eglwys Wen, Denbighshire

Welsh law to English. Some were in a position to dabble profitably in the great overseas adventures of the age. Thomas Myddelton, a successful merchant who became lord mayor of London, was able to accommodate his Denbighshire family with part-shares from £20 down to fifty shillings in his own investments in these ventures, on which profits could be as high as 400 or 500 per cent.

There were also less legitimate ways by which the gentry, especially those living near the coast, could line their pockets. Piracy was endemic all round the Welsh coast, and the gentry, even if they did not appear as principals, often provided the capital and the cover, including sometimes their own authority as commissioners in piracy. It was generally believed that misdeeds at sea, beginning quite legitimately as 'reprisals' against Spain, forced the last of the Griffiths of Penrhyn to forfeit the family's long primacy in North Wales.

The Irish plantations of Elizabeth and James I attracted many Welsh landlords as investors; a few made their homes there, but more stayed in Wales, often with a bigger income from their Irish than their Welsh estates. This helps to explain the slow response of Wales to the challenge of the New World. There was one notable exception. William Vaughan, a younger brother of one of these Irish adventurers, tried to relieve the poverty of his neighbours in west Wales by planting them in a colony he called Cambriol, in a corner of Newfoundland. But Cambriol never got over its

Cambriol, from John Mason's map of Newfoundland, 1625

teething troubles. Vaughan, if an able writer on colonial matters, lacked the robust temper which had enabled John Smith to rescue Virginia from a similar plight, and Cambriol soon became a mere memory.

Besides all this, there were ample opportunities for profitable investment in English business enterprises or at the bar (where Tudor and Stuart Welshmen did uncommonly well), or in the purchase of public office, and wide openings for enrichment in the service of great families, where the younger sons of the Welsh gentry are so often found in this age. This did not necessarily mean permanent severance from Wales, any more than did investment in Ireland. Success was often followed by retirement to the homeland, or at least the purchase of an estate for the next generation to settle there. The wider experience of men like these was an invaluable asset, and their wealth had a stimulating effect on the Welsh economy.

There were many clashes between the new business-minded landlords and their more conservative neighbours, as well as the small freeholders they were squeezing off the land. But the enclosure movement in England had no exact counterpart in Wales. Enclosure went on through the Tudor and Stuart periods, causing frequent complaints in court leet, civil suits at the assizes and even local riots, but the culprits were as often small freeholders, extending cultivation to land adjoining their holdings, as great landlords overstocking the mountain pastures with their flocks or with those of outsiders paying for pasturage. The interdependence of highland and lowland, and indeed the whole basis of local economy, were being undermined. Of actual eviction, deserted villages or the disappearance of former 'houses of husbandry'—the burden of so many English complaints—there is little sign. But it was the small man who felt most acutely the insecurity caused by the too rapid transition from Welsh to English legal concepts.

The most troublesome dispute flared up when Elizabeth's favourite, the earl of Leicester, as chief forester of the royal forest of Snowdon, was given a wide commission to investigate 'encroachments' on this royal preserve, where the red deer still ran wild. By far the biggest encroachments were on wide sheep-walks, annexed by men of substance, who could afford the fines and made an outward show of co-operation; it was the smaller freeholders, who had nibbled piecemeal at the moorlands adjoining their holdings, who became alarmed, till all Gwynedd was in an uproar. The religious conservatism of many of Leicester's opponents, while he posed as a champion of the establishment and most of his henchmen conformed to it, helped to sharpen the conflict. Eventually a compromise was reached, and the countryside quietened down until the issue was abortively raised once more under Charles I.

Sheep rearing was the main basis of the Welsh economy, but cattle were on the increase. The drover, conducting herds along well-marked tracks to Smithfield market or to midland pastures for fattening, was becoming a key man in rural society. He could not trade without a licence, and this was not granted unless he could give adequate financial guarantees. The return of the drovers marked one of the periods when money circulated freely. The menace of Irish competition in this field banded Welsh MPs together on several occasions in the seventeenth

A Welsh drover

century. Goats, a prolific source both of production and of destruction, appear to have mainly run wild; very rarely are they mentioned in farm inventories. The pig, at home in the town as well as the country, was generally kept for family consumption.

Although an older order persisted, the face of the land was changing perceptibly. The *gwely* was becoming a consolidated estate, with a central manor house embodying, both inside and out, the taste of the age, even to stone staircases, chimneys and glazed windows, and many of the smaller squires were straining or crippling their fortunes to vie with their wealthier neighbours. Bond hamlets, and even *hafotai* originally built as temporary summer shelters, were turning into compact farms, though in some parts the traditional use of the *hafoty* persisted up to the nineteenth century.

In the richer valleys and coastal plains mixed husbandry was practised and corn was grown for the market, often with the aid of hired labour; the uplands were a region of sheep farms

Plas Mawr, Conway, an Elizabethan gentleman's town house

where as a rule only the family was employed. With the *gwely* there disappeared the system of personal names that was so closely associated with it. By the fifteenth century Welsh *uchelwyr* with English family ties or legal dealings were beginning to abandon the use of patronymics (virtually abbreviated family trees) in favour of the English form of surname.

Industry and trade were still too feeble to bring into existence a distinct class of industrial employers or labourers; they were

Carding   *Spinning*

almost wholly ancillary to agriculture. The spinning and weaving of wool were widely practised in farming households and by the domestic staffs of great houses; in Merioneth and Montgomery the industry was more organized, thanks to an Elizabethan Act which gave the Shrewsbury Drapers' Company a sales monopoly for Welsh cloth. The rough cloth was taken by the country weavers to weekly markets, first at Oswestry then at Shrewsbury, to be finished for export by the skilled Shrewsbury shearmen. It meant, as a sympathetic observer later commented, that 'the Welsh had the labour and strangers the profit', and there was no advancement in the industry save by residence in Shrewsbury and membership of the privileged company, which maintained its monopoly, despite repeated efforts of London 'interlopers' to break it, till the mid-eighteenth century; but it also meant that the Welsh weaver had a protected market and was thus able to supplement what he could make from the land.

Mining was normally just a department of estate management carried on by the owner with his own labour force—helped out, perhaps, by an imported skilled miner or two; only occasionally were veins or seams leased to an outside adventurer. Lead was mined in Flintshire and Cardiganshire, copper near Neath, coal on the seaward fringes of both northern and southern coalfields and sometimes—from near the surface, for purely local use—farther inland. For of course coal could not be carried along the roads to be found in Wales

Weaving

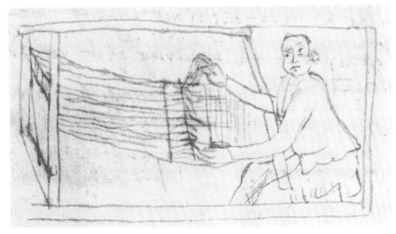

Shrewsbury market hall

without turning it to dust. Even near the Pembrokeshire coast a mine six or seven feet deep, from which the coal had to be hauled up in a barrel by four men turning a windlass, was a novel development. Similarly the roofing slates quarried by small working partnerships in Caernarvonshire only served local markets, unless the quarry stood conveniently near the sea.

Most of the coal that was mined went to feed the hearths of gentlemen's houses or to meet the small demands of black-smith, dyer or brewer. Charcoal was the agent for smelting metals—to the detriment of the forests and sometimes to the anger of commoners who resented the inroads on their cus-tomary source of fuel. In Elizabeth's day copper was smelted and manufactured near Neath, the Glamorgan iron industry was fostered under Sir Henry Sidney, and Worcestershire ironmasters were reaching out into Monmouthshire. But the biggest mining enterprises were promoted by two chartered companies, largely financed by German capital and manned by German skilled workers. The Company for the Mines Royal was given the right of mining for gold and silver, copper and lead, but they leased their Welsh rights to a succession of contractors, who opened up the Cardiganshire mines and sent substantial quantities of silver to the mint; early in the following century these were taken over by Thomas Myddelton's goldsmith brother Hugh. The Company for the Mineral and Battery Works was concerned with manufacture, and it was under patents issued by it that the wire works near Tintern abbey began their long career.

These industrial developments had a quickening effect on the seaports, especially those of South Wales. Increasing quantities of coal (and later of iron) were sent from Glamorgan across the Bristol Channel, or to France, and from Pembrokeshire to Ireland. Pembrokeshire was also the chief grain-producing county of Wales, helping to feed the less productive area of the Cardigan Bay coast and in bad years North Wales as well. The chief export of the Cardigan Bay ports was fish; Caernarvonshire had a brisk trade in slates to Ireland, between three and four thousand being exported during the decade following 1583. Imports to South Wales were chiefly luxuries

Caernarvon in 1610

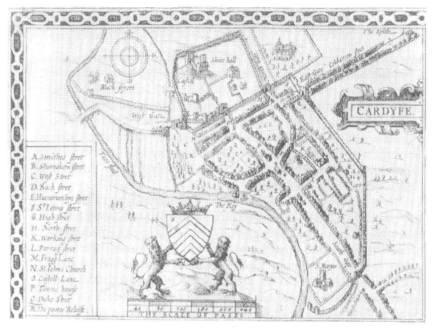

Cardiff in 1610

like wine and fruit; North Wales too depended largely on its coasting trade, not only for imported luxuries, but also for supplies of everyday goods like iron, soap and candles.

Only in the ports and market towns was there any approach to urban conditions. They contained perhaps ten per cent of the total population (of less than 300,000 in all), in towns ranging from two thousand inhabitants down to two hundred. Many of the gentry had houses in the larger towns, and their younger sons (especially now that primogeniture had become the rule) were often apprenticed there to trades or professions —unless their ambitions took them farther afield to London, or to seek their fortunes in the army and navy. Many Welsh soldiers—like Sir Roger Williams, the supposed original of Shakespeare's Fluellen—fought with the armies in the Low Countries, some for the Dutch, some for the Spanish, a few for both. Many, mainly from the Devereux country of south-west Wales, were in the service of the earl of Essex both in Ireland and abroad. Some of these rallied to him in his tragic bid for power at the close of the reign, when his Welsh steward, Sir Gely Meyrick, suffered with him on the block.

Throughout the Tudor period the old Wales and the new lived side by side, much as Celts and Romans had coexisted a thousand years earlier. On the one hand were the new legal and administrative structures, the new religious order, the land settlement and the advance of industry. On the other was the ancient tongue, still spoken almost everywhere except on official business, and now consciously fostered, in face of threats of disintegration and debasement, not only by professional bards but by scholars influenced by the European Renaissance and by religious zealots bent on expounding their faith to monoglot compatriots. In North Wales there were still formal sessions of the bards, presided over by the principal local gentry, where singers and poets received their various grades in the bardic order and competed for the honour of the silver harp in the gift of the Mostyns. Elizabeth authorized by royal proclamation an eisteddfod at Caerwys in Flintshire, but part of her purpose is made clear in the proclamation: to get rid of the 'intollerable multitude' of 'vagraunt and idle persons naming theim selfes minstrelles, rithmers and barthes', by means of tests which would separate the sheep from the goats.

After that the eisteddfod disappears underground till the national revival of the late eighteenth century. The chief Tudor bards handed on their lore to pupils, some of whom were retained as household bards (a practice surviving till nearly the end of the seventeenth century), while others scratched a living as freelances; but the art was in rapid decline. There was no flagging, however, in the output of more popular verse in the 'free' metres, nor of the still more amateurish folk drama, or *anterliwtiau*, which remained a normal feature of village feast days. But the *anterliwt* never attracted the interest of wealthy patrons and only rarely that of competent poets.

Yet the continental Renaissance was far from leaving Wales unaffected. For in the century following Henry VIII's reign, Welsh dictionaries, grammars and treatises on poetic diction flowed from Welsh humanists, with translations of classical works on a variety of learned themes. And so a more flexible and adaptable prose came into existence, of which the crowning achievement was the Welsh Bible. Some of these humanists

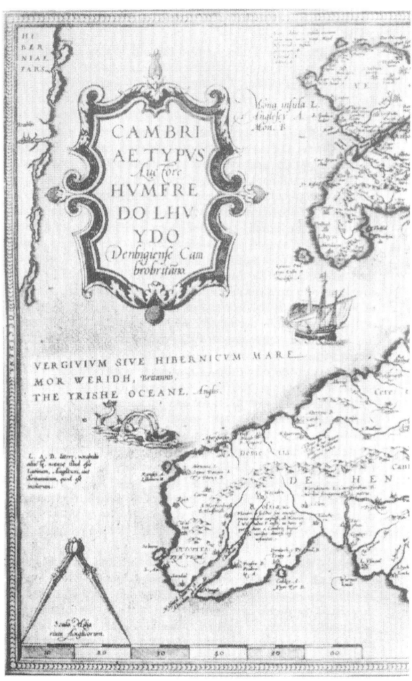

Llwyd's map of Wales, 1573

83

were also keen antiquaries, rummaging private libraries and those of dissolved monasteries for manuscript poems and chronicles. These activities led to the publication in 1584, by the chaplain to the then President of Wales and under his patronage, of a history of Wales which remained the basis of all writings in this field till the present century; another was the inclusion in the world atlas of the Dutch geographer Ortelius of the first map of Wales with any pretensions to accuracy, contributed by a physician and humanist of Denbigh.

By the mid-seventeenth century this renaissance had spent its force—to come to life again a century later. Most of the works written, translated or rediscovered by the Welsh humanists remained buried in manuscript for lack of patrons, and in default of printing, a small band of scribes laboriously produced handwritten copies of the works of bards and scholars, living and dead.

When the Welsh Tudors gave place to the Scottish Stuarts, the men who counted in Welsh life accepted with pride the name 'British'—with its echoes of Geoffrey of Monmouth—as a common denominator for the three nations inhabiting the island, but distinguished themselves (as the 'ancient inhabiters') from the 'usurpers and mere possessors' by the prefix 'Cambro-'. The loyalty the Tudors had fostered was inherited by their successors. Attempts to stir up disaffection among the recusants of the south-east, or to involve the Welsh in the Gunpowder Plot, only confirmed the general loyalty of the gentry. Henceforth Roman Catholic efforts were confined to quiet missionary activity, especially from the Jesuit centres—Holywell in Flintshire, and Cwm, just over the Herefordshire border.

The Acts of Union and the litigation and supplementary legislation arising out of them were ceasing to dominate the Welsh scene, and the Elizabethan settlement in religion had won general acceptance. The Welsh members were taking an increasingly effective part in Parliament, and contested elections were becoming more frequent. New issues in both politics and religion were overshadowing those which had dominated the last century.

Further Reading

David Williams, *Modern Wales*, 1950 (useful also for succeeding chapters).

Id., 'The Welsh Tudors', *History Today*, Feb. 1954.

W. Ll. Williams, *The Making of Modern Wales*, 1919.

W. Ogwen Williams, *Tudor Gwynedd*, 1958.

Id., 'The survival of the Welsh Language after the Union of England and Wales, 1536–1642', *Welsh Hist. Rev.*, ii, 1964.

Glanmor Williams, *Welsh Reformation Essays*, 1967.

J. M. Cleary, 'The Catholic resistance in Wales', *Blackfriars*, March 1957.

C. J. A. Skeel, *The Council in the Marches of Wales*, 1904.

Penry Williams, *The Council in the Marches of Wales under Elizabeth I*, 1958.

G. Dyfnallt Owen, *Elizabethan Wales*, 1962.

T. C. Mendenhall, *The Shrewsbury Drapers and the Welsh Wool Trade*, 1953.

A. H. Dodd, *Studies in Stuart Wales*, 1953 (2nd ed., 1971).

Joan Thirsk (ed.), *The Agrarian History of England and Wales*, iv (1500–1640), Chapters ii, vi and xi.

V

Educational and Religious Movements, 1630–1780

Towards the end of James I's reign an English Puritan wrote a book which he whimsically called *A Consolation for our Grammar Schools*. Its main purport was to promote 'the more speedie attaining of our English tongue' as the only effective means of reclaiming 'the ignorant country of Wales', as well as the Irish and the Red Indians, from 'their exceeding ignorance of our holy God and of all true and good learning'. Not that Wales herself was devoid of grammar schools: there were at the time three grammar schools in North Wales and at least twice as many in the south. The registers of four Cambridge colleges

Botwnnog church and school, founded 1616

for the early seventeenth century show pupils from eleven Welsh schools, and there had been a substantial Welsh colony at Oxford in Glyn Dŵr's day. The Inns of Court were even more widely patronized, whether for professional purposes or merely as 'finishing schools'. Why then all this talk about 'the ignorant country of Wales'?

The answer is, of course, that while a small minority was able to acquire fluency in English at grammar school or university, the vast majority spoke what was to English ears unintelligible gibberish. Worse still, it was rooted in pagan antiquity and fostered by a bardic order believed to be direct successors of the ancient Druids. An English member of one of James I's parliaments assured the House that the Welsh were 'an ydolotrous nation and worshippers of divells . . . thrust out into the mountains where they lived long like thiefs and robbers and are to this day the most base, peasantly, perfidious peoples of the world'.

Fortunately the Welsh in Wales and the English in England do not make up the whole picture: there were also the Welsh in London, thoroughly satisfied with the Tudor settlement but never forgetting their homeland. From this quarter there issued in 1630 the first portable edition of the Welsh Bible, bound up with the Welsh Prayer Book and a metrical version of the Psalms by the clerical bard Edmund Prys. The sponsors (among them Thomas Myddelton) were a group of Welsh Londoners, mostly of Puritan but not sectarian leanings, bent on living down this reproach of spiritual ignorance at home—men who saw the remedy, not in suppression of the language but in its extended use for religious enlightenment.

This spate of religious literature in clear, straightforward Welsh prose, must have helped to stimulate theological interest to an extent the Reformation itself had failed to achieve, but it certainly did not turn the Welsh into a nation of Puritans. Moralizing parsons declaimed against their addiction to 'playgrounds and bowls and taverns and football and tennis'—on Sundays too! An Anglesey squire's diary for the years just preceding the Civil War introduces us to a world, not of theology and introspection, but of horse-racing and cockfighting, wakes and village plays, dice and shuffleboard and tennis in the churchyard, with recurrent variations on the theme, 'Was drunk and lost my hat, God forgive me!'

There was some penetration of Puritanism along the border and in the southern coastal plain. The stricter enforcement of conformity when William Laud (previously bishop of St Davids) became archbishop of Canterbury in 1633, led to the ejection of refractory parsons at Cardiff and in the Swansea area. At Llanfaches in Monmouthshire there was formed in 1639 the first Puritan congregation in Wales, in close touch with the growing Puritanism of Bristol, but not yet fully separated from the establishment. Walter Cradock, a young curate ejected from Cardiff, found refuge at Wrexham, where his fiery sermons drew large crowds at six in the morning. Another of the ejected joined a party from Gloucester which emigrated in 1639 to the new Puritan colony on Massachusetts Bay, taking with him one or two of the neighbouring laity. But these were rare exceptions to the general acceptance of the Elizabethan order.

On the political plane the prevailing tone, both inside and outside the House of Commons, was equally compliant to royal policy. Naturally there was some resistance to Charles I's frequent and irregular raids on his subjects' pockets for the supplies his Parliaments were reluctant to vote him; but only rarely was there any hint of constitutional principle behind the protests. What was emphasized was the shortage of ready cash during the 'dead times' between the cattle sales.

It was natural that disaffection should be most marked in the seafaring shires of South Wales, for there the shortcomings of Buckingham's ministry were visible in crippled ships putting in to Milford Haven from his unhappy warlike adventures, or the interruption by freebooters of peaceful traffic with Ireland and France. A telling indication of the state of popular feeling is seen in a wild rumour, hatched in Carmarthenshire in 1628 and spreading like wildfire through Gower and across the Channel to Cornwall, that the guileless young king had been poisoned by his evil genius, Buckingham.

Soon after this a new presidency of Wales, that of the border earl of Bridgwater, was inaugurated at Ludlow by the first performance of Milton's *Comus*, with its tribute to the 'old and

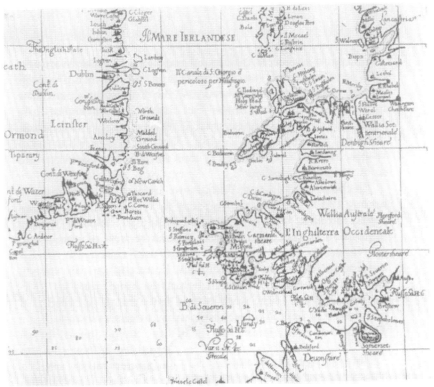

The Irish sea

haughty nation, proud in arms' over which he was to rule. But spirits were soon damped again. Bridgwater fell ill, and his council, starved of supplies, was unable to cope with its work. Ship money, with which the king hoped to plug the gaping hole in his finances, raised no outcry in Wales since it was being used for coastal defence; but the fifth successive levy coincided with the raising of a costly force of two thousand men — the largest raised in Wales since the Union — to deal with the uprising Charles had brought on by his ham-fisted dealings with the Scots. Bridgwater, returning to Ludlow after a prolonged absence, found an alarmingly 'altered disposition' which he attributed to 'pretending patriots who have taught too many to speak of the parliamentary way and legality of proceeding'.

A further cause of unrest was the growing suspicion that hidden influences at court were bent on selling out to Rome.

The favours shown to influential recusants like the Marquess of Worcester and his son at Raglan bred rumours of a proposed 'Welsh popish army' to overthrow the Protestant cause, now fighting for its life in Europe. But the Welsh contingent duly marched north, its progress marred by no more serious incident than the inability of an English officer to get on with Welsh troops, so that he could 'never look for quietness between the soldiers and their officer'.

Elections to the Long Parliament aroused unusual interest among the Welsh gentry, and sent to Westminster an exceptional number who took a critical line in debates. But as opposition to the court moved beyond redress of immediate grievances to open attacks on crown and episcopate, Welsh opinion rallied to the establishment. From county after county came loyal declarations which, when the king raised his standard in August 1642, were turned into troops of horse and companies of foot. Against this loyalty, attempts to recruit for Parliament could make no headway; such opposition as remained in Wales had to go underground until it had the backing of parliamentary forces from without.

The 1st Marquess of Worcester

That is why the English civil war took the familiar form, for Wales, of successive invasions across Offa's Dyke. Until its third year the impact on Wales was limited to periodic levies to fight the king's battles in England, requisitions in money and in kind to support them, a close watch on the more vulnerable crossings from England, and, worst of all, the interruption of the cattle trade with London.

It was only in the extreme south-west, where Milford Haven gave shelter to parliamentary shipping, that the Roundhead cause, backed by the house of Devereux, could maintain any lasting foothold.

General Sir Thomas Myddelton

The first pitched battle on Welsh soil was fought in the autumn of 1644, when a Roundhead force under Sir Thomas Myddelton, the lord mayor's son, established itself at Montgomery. Welsh troops were recalled from England, local trainbands drilled, and castles, neglected since the Wars of the Roses, were hastily repaired and manned for the king. But, after his defeat at Naseby his control of Wales gradually crumbled. He took refuge at Raglan, and gathering what forces he could, he led them across the central uplands only to see them defeated outside Chester, which fell to Parliament early in 1646.

The way was now clear for a parliamentary invasion to cut him off from Welsh supplies and from communication with Ireland. The castles—built to subdue the surrounding countryside, not to resist invasion—proved no obstacle: they were by-passed and left to be reduced at leisure. The war in North Wales rapidly became a struggle in an impoverished countryside between rival bands of English soldiers ready to 'raven and spoyle all the country over', and sometimes (the lady of Gwydir complained) 'very rude'. Everywhere there were defections among the local gentry. By the summer of 1646 the whole of North Wales, except one or two of the more defensible castles, had submitted to Parliament, while in the south a force

Raglan castle, forty years after the siege

from Pembrokeshire swept away resistance in the south-eastern shires, until Raglan itself fell to assault, and its octogenarian owner was hauled off to die in the Tower. The renewal of fighting in 1648, when the Devereux faction changed sides, brought Cromwell himself into South Wales; a belated effort to reanimate the Royalist cause in North Wales won only limited support and was soon crushed.

Material damage in Wales was relatively small, except where the precincts of a castle were swept by artillery, a farmhouse or

Pembroke castle

mansion reduced to flames, or a church looted or desecrated. The castles had had their last taste of warfare: some were deliberately blown up to destroy their military value; others, where they did not return to residential use, suffered from neglect and gradual pillage, to follow the abbeys into the limbo of romantic ruins. There had been a good deal of sporadic cattle-raiding, but little or no destruction of crops or stock, and the drovers received handsome compensation from Parliament for their losses. The war had little of the savagery that marked the religious wars in Germany: opposing commanders would conclude their letters to each other, 'Your poore kinsman and ould play-fellow to serve you', or 'Your true friend as far as truth and loyalty will give him leave'. Savagery was reserved for the Irish who came over to help the king; those captured at Conway were thrown into the sea and 'sent by water to their own country'.

Nor was there any significant shift in the distribution of wealth or the balance of society. Those who had dipped into their fortunes in the king's cause were often able to retrieve them by exploiting the mineral wealth of their estates; others escaped the rigour of parliamentary fines through friends or kinsmen in the other camp, or by coming to terms with Parliament in the nick of time. The worst hit were the small royalist squires without capital or friends at court, but most of them contrived to cling on to what was left of their estates till after the Restoration. A few new fortunes were made and new county families founded by local men rising from obscurity through the spoils of office, or by Roundhead soldiers from England marrying Welsh heiresses and settling on their estates. The county committees through which Parliament exercised its authority during the Interregnum all contained a leavening of these new men, but there was also a sufficient nucleus of established families to preserve some outward continuity.

Most pervasive in its effects on Welsh life was the setting up of the Commission for the Propagation of the Gospel in Wales — the climax, though not the conclusion, of the missionary campaigns of English Puritans. The prejudice against the Welsh language for this purpose had already begun to break down when the Long Parliament employed Walter Cradock to preach to the Welsh prisoners brought to London after Naseby—partly in hopes of turning them into a Puritan nucleus when they went home, partly, no doubt, to distract them from such disorders as occurred later among Welsh troops in Cornwall when they celebrated St David's Day not wisely but too well. The commission, with a strong border element in its composition, was given wide control over the revenues of the Welsh Church. These funds were to be used to replace unacceptable incumbents by others conforming to Puritan standards, to finance itinerant preachers and to set up in every market town a grammar school under Puritan auspices. A further design of establishing in Wales 'a Colledge or two' for Welsh students was discussed by some of the commissioners, but never got off the ground.

Apart from this unrealized aim, the establishment of a Puritan parochial ministry was the least successful of the commissioners' efforts. It was easy enough to turn out several hundred unacceptable parsons, but far harder to find acceptable replacements; the result was that many livings were left vacant, and in many more the existing incumbent was left to carry on, or restored after ejection, without too rigid an insistence on Puritan standards. The effects of the itinerant ministry are harder to gauge. That there was a genuine religious revival in some parts, anticipating many of the better-known revivals of the eighteenth and nineteenth centuries, seems to be well-attested—among others by Cromwell when he declared (in a classic mixed metaphor) that 'God did kindle a seed there hardly to be paralleled since the primitive time'. For the commission was able to employ others besides Cradock who could move congregations in eloquent Welsh. One of the most influential—Morgan Llwyd, grandson of an Elizabethan soldier bard of Merioneth—was also a powerful writer of Welsh prose. His colleague, the more politically-minded Vavasour Powel, was one of the chief agents in Wales of the dominant Puritan faction, until he fell foul of Cromwell.

At least forty, perhaps as many as sixty grammar schools were set up by the commissioners. Very little is known about them, for in a few years they were swept away by the Restoration. Equally ephemeral was the attempt to impose a Puritan character on the Welsh Church. Some fifty of the intruded ministers were ejected at the Restoration; most of the rest conformed. A few Dissenting congregations, mainly in the borderland and the southern plain where Puritan influences had first seeped in, survived to lead a hunted existence under the Clarendon Code, until the Toleration Act of 1689.

Most severe of all was the persecution of the Quakers, who had first appeared in Wales towards the end of the Protectorate. Visits by George Fox had left little bands of disciples, and after the death of Morgan Llwyd, a number of those he had influenced passed over into Quakerism, which had many points of affinity with his teaching. When William Penn's 'Holy Experiment' in Pennsylvania opened a prospect of relief, groups

The Welsh Tract, Pennsylvania

from at least six Welsh counties negotiated with the founder for the purchase of thirty thousand acres in the new colony, and it is estimated that from 1682 till the end of the century some two thousand Welsh families went out there. It was the first substantial migration from Wales to the New World; but at home Quakerism languished in the course of the next century.

Indeed Wales, for long after the Restoration, remained firmly attached to the established order in Church, state and society. But although itinerant evangelism was 'out' and the Puritan schools were closed, there were still friends of Wales in London who hoped to achieve the same ends by a renewed educational drive. In 1674 Thomas Gouge, an ejected London minister, with the help of half a dozen Welsh ministers similarly situated, financial support from some Puritan merchants, and the patronage of a few 'broad church' bishops, founded the Welsh Trust.

Its main activity was the distribution of religious literature in translation. Schools were set up in which boys and girls were taught to read and tḥe boys to write and 'cast accompts' as well. Although the literature issued by the Trust was in Welsh, the children were taught through English to get them used to the language; this inevitably limited its usefulness in Welsh-speaking areas. Soon there were well over eighty of these schools, providing for about twenty children each, except in the larger towns and the smaller villages. Altogether more than fifteen hundred children were believed to have passed through them, but the number was already dwindling by 1678, and after Gouge's death three years later the movement declined rapidly.

Many were alienated by its Dissenting associations, especially in the overcharged political atmosphere of Charles II's later years, when the faction bent on excluding the King's popish brother found some violent adherents in South Wales, and the 'popish plot' scare resulted in the scattering of the Jesuit community at Cwm and the hounding to death of fourteen or fifteen harmless priests. The hobnobbing of South Wales opposition leaders with local Dissent revived old Civil War hatreds, and the Welsh Trust felt the backwash. But Wales as a whole remained loyal, and demonstrated this when the new President, the duke of Beaufort (the Protestant heir to Raglan) went on an impressive official 'progress' of the Principality near the close of the reign. This attachment to the throne weathered James II's reign; offers of help against William of Orange kept reaching him from Wales until he decided on flight. Then the Revolution of 1688 was accepted quietly but without enthusiasm.

Salute to Duke of Beaufort, Pembrokeshire, 1684

The Welsh Trust helped to pave the way for its more effective successor, the Society for Promoting Christian Knowledge, founded in 1699. This was a nation-wide movement initiated in the Church, and free from Dissenting associations. Some of its chief supporters came from Wales or the border; two were grandsons of Puritan commissioners of 1650, and others had worked for the Trust of 1674.

Like its predecessors, the SPCK made itself responsible for the dissemination of subsidized religious literature in Welsh, including two reprints of the Welsh Bible. Like them it set up schools—nearly a hundred by 1727—but it also made provision for teaching in Welsh-speaking areas, especially in North Wales, to be in Welsh. It suffered from the current political and theological divisions—this time from the strife between High and Low Church and between Jacobite and Hanoverian. No new schools were set up after 1727, and those already in existence were often sparsely and irregularly attended because (in the words of the dean of Bangor), 'their poverty is so great that they cannot allow themselves time to learn', the children being taken from school in summer to bring in the harvest and in winter to beg for bread.

Out of the SPCK in Wales, however, sprang the most effective weapon so far forged in the campaign against illiteracy. Griffith Jones, an earnest and tremendously energetic clergyman from Carmarthenshire with experience of teaching in an SPCK school, developed from about 1750 the idea of 'Circulating schools' which should move from parish to parish at three-monthly intervals—long enough, it was hoped, to enable the pupils to spell out the Bible and the catechism for themselves. Nothing more was attempted—not even the teaching of English to Welsh-speaking children.

The Circulating schools avoided many of the pitfalls into which the SPCK had fallen. By meeting in the winter they kept clear of the demand for child labour in the harvest; they also opened for three or four hours in the evening to meet the needs of the many who could not attend in the day, thus blazing the trail for adult education. Jones himself prepared his less experienced teachers by a 'crash' course of a few weeks —a foretaste of the pupil-teacher system of a century later. These dedicated young men then set about their task for two guineas a quarter or even less. By the time of Griffith Jones's death in 1761 nearly 3,500 schools had come and gone and nearly sixteen thousand pupils had passed through them—a substantial crack in the hard shell of illiteracy.

Jones was fortunate in his friends and supporters. The SPCK helped with books, and one of its pioneers, Sir John Philipps of Picton in Pembrokeshire, found him a living and gave him powerful protection against his many detractors. 'Madam' Bevan, wife of a local M.P., not only placed her fortune at the disposal of the schools, but kept them going for

Sir John Philipps   *Howel Harris*

eighteen years after Griffith Jones's death and made provision in her will for their indefinite continuance. To Griffith Jones, however, education was never more than a means to personal salvation. He made himself unpopular with authority by reviving itinerant evangelism, 'going about preaching', his bishop complained, 'on week days in Churches, Churchyards, and sometimes on the mountains to hundreds of auditors'.

A convert made by him in the neighbouring county of Cardigan—Daniel Rowland, curate of Llangeitho—and a Breconshire layman named Howel Harris, whom Griffith Jones had recruited for his Circulating schools, both independently followed suit in 1735. As a result Harris failed to obtain ordination and Rowland remained all his life a curate. Three years later William Williams, a student at the neighbouring Dissenting academy, also came under the influence of Harris, abandoned Dissent for Anglican ordination, and joined the evangelistic campaign. He is best known by the name of his wife's farm, Pantycelyn, where he lived between his missionary journeys.

In this region of Wales the extreme poverty which inhibited so many of the local clergy from effectively ministering to their scattered flocks had bred a sort of 'do-it-yourself' religion, expressing itself in informal gatherings and religious ditties sung to popular tunes. Religious revival was in the air, awaiting only inspired leadership. Pantycelyn, in an elegy on the death of Daniel Rowland over fifty years later, describes how when this 'Boanerges' preached to great crowds on the coming Judgement, 'wonder, fear and panic overtook great and small, every countenance changed, and knees trembled at the thunder'—nor was this all poetic exaggeration, as many eye-witnesses testified. Pantycelyn represents another side of the movement. Between 1744 and 1791 he published nearly ninety collections of Welsh hymns of his own composition, from penny broadsheets to substantial volumes, to say nothing of longer poems and prose works. His hymns—sung, surprisingly, in unison, to any familiar or easily-memorized tune—became as powerful a factor as Rowland's or Harris's sermons.

The supreme organizer, however, was Howel Harris. From 1736 he gave the movement permanence by gathering his converts into religious 'societies' after the pattern of those which had appeared in the English Church for the past seventy years, and had latterly been fostered by Moravian missionaries. Each had its lay leader or *cynghorwr*, and above them was gradually built an elaborate regional super-structure, broadly pres-byterian in character but within the establishment. Harris was almost as tire-less a traveller as Wesley: it was he who carried the torch into the south-east and into North Wales, though here the move-ment long remained de-pendent on the fount of inspiration in the south.

MS of a hymn of Pantycelyn

Rowland, for his part, was generally content to let the mountain come to Mahomet, and Llangeitho long remained the Mecca to which ardent disciples resorted even from the north, braving the buffetings of storms at sea and hostile mobs by land.

It was Harris, too, who first contacted Wesley and Whitefield, leaders of the parallel movement in England. The nickname 'Methodist' was applied to both; but when in 1742 the two English leaders parted company on the great issue of Predestin-

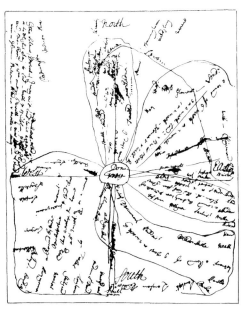

Howel Harris's diagram of his travels

ation and Free Grace, the Welsh followed Whitefield and became Calvinistic Methodists, Wesley tacitly agreeing to leave the Welsh-speaking areas to the ministrations of Harris. The Welsh Methodists encountered the same sort of hostility as Wesley's missionaries met in England; they were obnoxious to the church courts as men who undermined ecclesiastical discipline, and to the lay authorities because by collecting crowds they invited breaches of the peace. The view of the man in the street was coloured by vague memories of Roundhead oppression in his grandfather's day, as appears in epithets like 'Cradocks and Roundheads' (or their Welsh equivalents) so often hurled at them.

The full impact of the Methodist Revival was not felt until the close of the century, when the movement ceased to be merely regional and became nationwide; but some incidental effects were already asserting themselves. The hymns of Pantycelyn and the sermons of the great preachers were giving a new lease of life to Welsh for the expression of less ephemeral matters than those contained in popular almanacs and street ballads. Equally important for the future was the emergence of new leaders within Wales itself.

London, however, still remained an essential central focus for many Welsh movements. For example, the Honourable Society of Cymmrodorion, founded in 1751, 'for the encouragement of literature, science and art as connected with Wales', had its headquarters in London, but there were 'corresponding members' distributed through all thirteen shires of the principality, and the initiative came from a remarkable group of men from small Anglesey farmsteads: the versatile Morris brothers and their neighbour Goronwy Owen, rejuvenator of Welsh classical verse. The Cymmrodorion sponsored the publication of books in Welsh or about Wales, indulged in not very well-informed speculation about Welsh antiquities and philology, put up money to secure in the ecclesiastical court a verdict (not always observed in practice in later years) against the appointment of a monoglot English parson to a monoglot Welsh parish, and supported Welsh charities and schemes for the economic benefit of the land—along with many more ambitious but unfulfilled projects. Its meetings, held in London taverns, were often of too convivial a character to commend the Cymmrodorion to the Methodists.

So in the third quarter of the eighteenth century Welsh energies were flowing in two distinct channels; a third, which was purely economic in character, was just beginning to gather strength.

Further Reading

G. F. Nuttall, *The Welsh Saints, 1640–60*, 1957.
Mary Clements, *The S.P.C.K. and Wales*, 1954.
Erasmus Saunders, *A View of the State of Religion in the Diocese of St David's*, 1721, repr. 1949.
F. A. Cavenagh, *Griffith Jones*, 1930.
G. F. Nuttall, *Howel Harris, 1714–73: the Last Enthusiast*, 1965.
L. Twiston Davies and Averil Edwards, *Welsh Life in the Eighteenth Century*, 1959.

VI

Economic Development
1700–1850

The religious and educational revival culminating in Methodism was an indigenous movement responding to emotional
tides over much of western Europe; but the economic developments which followed owed their impetus mainly to fashions
originating in England, and transplanted into Wales either by
force of example or by direct 'colonization'. To a great extent
agriculture and industry marched together, but since most of
the Welsh were employed on the land, it will be convenient to
start from there.

A gentleman-farmer of western Caernarvonshire, writing
during the Napoleonic period, described farming practice half
a century earlier in words which could have been echoed in
most parts of Wales except the richer valleys:

No ground was then fallowed, no pease, grass, turnips or
potatoes raised, no cattle fattened and little grain sold. Oats
and barley were alternately sown, and during seven months
of the year the best soil was ravaged by flocks of sheep, a
certain number of which were annually sold and carried off
to be fed in richer pastures. . . . When seed time was finished,
the plough and harrow were laid aside till autumn, and the
sole employment of the farmer consisted in weeding his corn
fields and in digging and conveying home peat, turf and
heath for winter fuel. The produce of a farm . . . was barely
sufficient to pay the trifling rent and the servants' wages
and to procure his family a scanty subsistence.

An 18th century plough, Pembrokeshire

Apart from wretched communications and the poverty of much of the soil, Welsh agriculture suffered from lack of leadership. Many of the bigger estates had dropped, through marriage settlements, into the laps of absentee English owners, while the small owner lacked the capital for the sort of improvement now spreading through agrarian England.

There were exceptions, even in the more backward shires. Thomas Johnes, a collateral descendant of Sir Rhys ap Thomas, spent lavishly on stock-breeding experiments, afforestation, better farmhouses and the introduction of new crops on his Cardiganshire estates, and he passed on his experience to his tenants in a book published with a Welsh translation; but he was a scholar who had studied at Edinburgh. In Anglesey, a few enterprising farmers had for more than a century made successful trials of the island's abundant limestone, when they could get coal to burn it; or, by the seashore, of sand rich in shells. Henry Rowlands, an able clerical antiquary, described these experiments and their scientific basis in a valuable treatise written (but not published) in 1704. A brother parson learned something of the advanced agriculture of Herefordshire during residence as chancellor of the diocese, and applied it on his own Anglesey estate by adopting turnip culture—to such effect that by 1737 the crop was taking nearly a month to hoe. In most of Wales, however, lack of winter fodder meant that when November set in there was a wholesale slaughter for salting down among the stock left after the sales.

During the second half of the century attempts were made to remedy Welsh backwardness through county agricultural societies which offered premiums for good farming. But it was the wartime shortages imposed by the struggle with France that brought Wales into line with the Agrarian Revolution. 'Spirited proprietors' imbued with the new ideas appeared in county after county. Some organized huge agricultural meetings for tenants and neighbours in emulation of the Holkham sheep-shearings; others employed bailiffs experienced in the new methods, or kept their tenants up to scratch by replacing long leases by short ones carrying restrictive clauses, or else by year-to-year tenancies. Afforestation became a popular hobby with such as could afford it, to make good some of the spoliation of the woodlands of Powys and Gwent (for example) by sales of timber to the navy or by the depredations of the charcoal-burner.

The efforts of these benefactors were encouraged by awards from the Society of Arts; but far more important was the work of the Board of Agriculture founded, with a government subsidy, at the very outset of the war. It was under its auspices that the Montgomeryshire parson Walter Davies, known in Wales by his bardic name Gwallter Mechain, published two detailed critical reports on agriculture in North and South Wales respectively. He was convinced that part of the answer to food shortages lay in better use of the extensive waste lands of Wales, especially the upland commons. This called for a planned effort, instead of piecemeal encroachment, to enclose for individual exploitation lands hitherto used in common, thus opening the way to scientific breeding and tillage or development of mining or quarrying. Only a private Act of Parliament could give the necessary compulsory powers. Such Acts, common in England from early in the century, eventually reached the borderland of Wales, chiefly for schemes of drainage too expensive for the individual owner or for the redistribution of arable strips in the lowlands. After the outbreak of the French Revolutionary wars enclosure reached the heartland,

Draining Traeth Mawr, 1806

and cultivation crept to unheard-of heights up the mountains, which became interlaced with the familiar drystone walls.

Apart from the effects on agriculture, enclosure contributed much to the improvement of land transport. The most notable case was the draining of Traeth Mawr, the inlet of the sea which divides Caernarvonshire from Merioneth. This greatly facilitated travel over north-western Wales, and it was fitting that the two new centres of population which sprang up on the drained land—Portmadoc and Tremadoc—should be named after the author of the scheme, W. A. Madocks, who ruined himself over it. He was a rare exception. Generally the big landowners were the men who profited most; the small free-holder less so, since he could not meet the costs involved. The movement thus tended to widen still further the gap between greater and lesser gentry.

The man on whom enclosure bore hardest, however, was the cottager who had relied on supplementing his meagre wages by keeping a pig or two on the common, or finding there the brushwood, furze or peat he needed for heating. Worse still, many of them, with the encouragement of the parish authorities, had built their cottages on waste land they had themselves cleared after the day's work, under the mistaken impression that there was legal force behind the tradition that if a man built a cabin in a day and a night, so that smoke could be seen issuing from the chimney next morning, it became his freehold. But the tide of opinion was turning against the squatter: 'If this was permitted to go on we should soon be reduced to the miserable condition of the sister kingdom . . . and universal poverty would be the consequence.' And so whole groups of cottagers found themselves evicted. Enclosure often provoked serious riots, leading to transportation of the ringleaders, but on one occasion, in 1826, the squatters won by more peaceable methods, thanks to powerful friends in London.

Sample labourers' budgets collected by philanthropic investigators, on the eve of the war, show families of six to eight unable even then to make them balance. Annual earnings in each case hovered round £20—a little more when the eldest boy, at thirteen, could contribute a trifle, a little less when all were too young to earn. The bulk of this was swallowed up in barley or oat meal, butter, milk, bread and potatoes, leaving nothing to meet the £5 or £6 incurred annually for rent, clothes, fuel and lighting.

Industrial development at home and emigration overseas were slow to take effect, and there was no outlet for an expanding rural population except employment as farm labourers. Rarely met with in Tudor days, this class was now increasing to the point where even in the uplands labourers might average out at two per farm. The children of the small farmer often had to work in this capacity (for little more than their keep) either on the parental holding or with a neighbour. The ranks of agricultural labour were further swollen by the tendency of landlords to add farm to farm, leaving many smallholders on the labour market; and of course the spread of year-to-year tenancies made this easier. There was thus a ruinous competition for both farms and cottages, with a corresponding rise in rents.

All this, added to the burden of high indirect taxation and scarcity prices, made life desperately hard for the little man on the land. But peace brought no relief. The agricultural depression into which England was plunged from the end of the war to the opening of Victoria's reign hit Wales even harder by reason of the prevalence there of the smallholder, who felt the impact most severely. The extension of cultivation up the mountainside, or the heavy costs of procuring an allotment under an enclosure award, might be an economic proposition while prices were high, but the post-war slump wiped out the speculative profits and reduced many a farmer to bankruptcy. If the rick-burnings under 'Captain Swing' which agitated the south of England in the early 1830s found few imitators in Wales, this was partly because the farmer was in little better plight than the labourer, partly because of Methodist exhortations to patience in adversity and obedience to authority.

Welsh industry, like Welsh agriculture, remained in a state of arrested development until the eighteenth century brought changes which accelerated with the succession of wars from 1740 onwards. The Cardiganshire lead mines, under Hugh Myddelton's successor, had reached a point where enough silver was separated to procure him a licence from Charles I to mint it at Aberystwyth; but the Civil War called a halt to this as to many other industrial advances, till the Revolution of 1688 ushered in the age of competition in mining. Copper mines lost their position as 'mines royal', even when gold was found in them, and soon afterwards the Company for the Mines Royal was deprived of its monopoly. Mining rights henceforth depended on a licence from the owner of the soil, and there was a scramble among both owners and adventurers to exploit the mineral wealth of Wales.

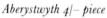

Aberystwyth 4/– piece

Cwmsymlog lead mine, Cardiganshire, 1670

Towards the end of the seventeenth century a fresh attack was made on the Cardiganshire mines by Humphry Mackworth. Through his wife, Mackworth had acquired property in Neath, including a lease of the coal which the burgesses had hitherto worked in small individual pits. This he was able to use for smelting his ores from coal-less Cardiganshire. The enterprise called for a bigger force of skilled labour than could be supplied locally, so Mackworth sent for recruits to his native Shropshire; he even used convict labour. True to the principles of the SPCK (of which he was a founding member), he paid a local schoolmaster £30 a year to teach the workmen's children. But his Cardiganshire venture set the county by the ears and petered out in lawsuits and recriminations which reached the House of Commons.

The wave of mining speculation also had its impact on Flintshire and the neighbouring parts of Denbighshire. Here there was abundance of lead ore, some of it silver-bearing, which had been spasmodically mined and smelted since Roman times, and there were handy creeks for export. But from the end of the seventeenth century a more systematic attack was made on the richer seams, and greater advantage taken of the local coal. Vast fortunes were made; but here, as in Cardiganshire, litigation was apt to run away with the profits, and as mines grew deeper, drainage problems became correspondingly acute. The Newcomen 'atmospheric' pump was in use in Flintshire within a few years of its invention in 1705. In Cardiganshire, towards the middle of the century, some of the principal landowners objected to attempts to claim as crown land areas they had hoped to mine for lead, and they did not scruple to incite to riot the workmen engaged by the crown agent, Lewis Morris, one of the trio of Anglesey brothers to whom the contemporary revival of Welsh culture owed so much.

Far more important were the developments in the iron industry which began soon after this and reached their climax under the impetus of war. In the seventeenth century coal had come into general use for smelting copper and lead, wherever it could conveniently be mined, but iron smelting remained dependent on the extravagant agency of charcoal until in 1709 the Quaker ironmaster Abraham Darby made in Shropshire his first successful experiments in smelting with coke. A dozen years later the process was extended by a Montgomeryshire fellow-Quaker, Charles Lloyd, to a charcoal furnace he was

Flintshire coal mine, 1684

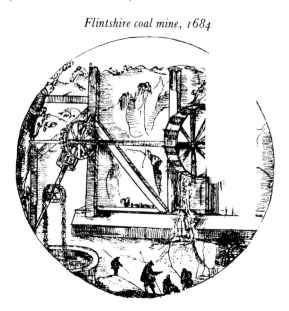

Wilkinson's ironworks, Bersham, c. *1800*

working at Bersham, in the heart of the coal and ironstone
district of east Denbighshire. But it was under his successors
Isaac Wilkinson and his more successful son John—immigrants
from Cumbria—that Bersham reached the peak of its prosperity as a centre for cannon boring and the manufacture of
cylinders for the Boulton and Watt steam engine.

By this time the wars with France were creating a boundless
demand for munitions, and English adventurers were flocking
into areas of Wales where the iron industry might be profitably
developed. In 1759 Isaac Wilkinson, with partners, took a
favourable lease of some rugged and undeveloped land near
the hamlet of Merthyr Tudful, with abundant woodlands at
hand and the Dowlais brook to provide the water power.
Next year they engaged an experienced manager from Shropshire, John Guest, who replaced charcoal by coke, became a
partner in this and in other ventures of his own in the area,
and founded a dynasty which by his grandson's time con-
trolled the whole enterprise, with an army of a thousand coal
miners raising 1,400 tons daily, another thousand in the ironstone mines, and 2,500 in his 180 furnaces.

Just after the Seven Years' War Anthony Bacon, a London
merchant dealing in coal and iron, leased another tract, rich
in coal and ironstone, a little farther west, and developed the
great Cyfarthfa ironworks. The outbreak of war with America
led to profitable munition contracts, and when he died he left
£1,500,000. His successor—Richard Crawshay, a runaway

Yorkshire boy who had done well in the hardware trade in London—was similarly helped to fortune by the wars with France which began in 1793. Crawshay founded another dynasty of ironmasters, which remained in control till the end of the last century. These were the first works in Britain to make wrought iron by the improved puddling process which was to revolutionize the industry. Indeed the 'Welsh method', as it came to be called, was in part the brain-child of a Cyfarthfa foreman.

The new industrial belt centred in Merthyr extended for some eighteen miles along the northern rim of the coalfield, eastward into Monmouthshire and westward into Carmarthenshire. The new capitalists came mainly from England, but most of the workmen came from the adjacent countryside—at first seasonally, leaving their families to look after their holdings at home, then as permanent residents, expanding Merthyr into a sprawling, insanitary town of over seven thousand inhabitants—the largest in Wales by the time of the first census. It was still the largest in 1861, with a population which had reached fifty thousand and was drawn from much farther afield; for the demand for labour kept growing, and Merthyr—a town in size but a village in government—became a haven for misfits, even from rural North Wales at the height of the unrest caused by enclosure. By the end of the Napoleonic Wars, South Wales was contributing about a third of the iron production of Great Britain, and early in Victoria's reign production was extended westward into the area of anthracite coal, which new inventions were making available to the iron industry.

Meanwhile in east Denbighshire coal and iron were creating a cluster of grimy colliery villages. But only the stronger units weathered the crisis of 1825–6, and fewer still were able to take advantage of the railway boom or to equip themselves for the improved processes of the fifties. When George Borrow was walking in the neighbourhood on an inky night in 1854, he found his way with the aid of three immense glares from three different ironworks, but they were lone survivors; the North Wales iron industry now counted for little in the economy of Wales, and still less in that of Britain.

Cyfarthfa ironworks, 1811

During the same period the copper and brass industries were also expanding, and they too were reaching out for the mineral resources of Wales. The Bristol manufacturers were within easy reach by sea of both the ores of Cornwall and the coal of South Wales, and the three areas had long been closely linked. In the course of the eighteenth century Swansea, with its superior shipping facilities, superseded Neath as a centre of the copper industry, but the Midland manufacturers looked nearer home. In Flintshire the Holywell district offered the

Padley's wharf, Swansea, 1827

Parys Mountain, 1785

advantages of plentiful water power, access to navigable waters and an urban population which by the time of the first census had reached five thousand. Towards the middle of the eighteenth century a Cheadle company was using it for brass manufacture, and in the following decade the highlands of Snowdonia were being scoured by prospectors for the copper ore they had long been known to conceal. The owners of the soil either joined in the scramble or let their minerals on lease to English manufacturers. But the decisive moment came in 1764, when the ores of Parys Mountain in Anglesey, known to the Romans but eluding later prospectors, were at last successfully tapped. What came to light was later remembered as 'nearly one unmixed mass of copper ore', near the surface and involving no heavy expense in sinking and draining.

After some twenty years of rapidly rising output, providing employment for twelve to fifteen hundred men, women and children, each of the two main proprietors of Parys Mountain

Neath coal works, 1798

formed a separate partnership to exploit his own ores, but
both employed as manager an Anglesey lawyer, Thomas
Williams, who proved an exceptionally able man of business—
in fact one of the very few outstanding native Welsh entre-
preneurs of the age. After a vigorous war with the Cornish
miners and the Birmingham manufacturers, Williams could
claim by 1800 to be conducting, through numerous subsidiary
and interlocking companies, half the copper industry of
Britain. Some ores were smelted on the spot, but the great
bulk was shipped away from Amlwch to Swansea, to Lancashire or nearer at hand to Holywell. In all three areas the
companies had their own works, and the men were paid in
the employers' own copper tokens.

   The use of copper by the navy for bolts and sheathing from
1761, and the vital part played by shipping in the American
and French Wars, came at a fortunate moment for the Welsh
copper industry. Naturally it was South Wales, with its well-
established coal and iron industries, export facilities and
industrial labour force, that reaped the principal benefit.
Copper created a new industrial area along the coast of

Glamorgan, extending some twenty miles on either side of Swansea, to match the iron empire in the north centred on Merthyr. Within this area new works kept springing up until 1830, established by immigrants from Cornwall, Worcestershire and elsewhere, till it was estimated that nineteen-twentieths of the ore produced in Great Britain was smelted here. Swansea harbour had to be enlarged in 1791, and the town doubled its population in the thirty years after the first census, though it did not catch up with Merthyr, which trebled itself in the same period. Holywell kept growing, too: its population had doubled itself by mid-century, but its industries had by then ceased to grow, and they were soon in decline. The death in 1801 of Thomas Williams, the master-mind of the whole industry, followed by the exhaustion of the most accessible veins on Parys Mountain, marked the end of this prosperous phase in the industrial history of North Wales.

The reaction against monopoly which triggered off the revolution in the heavy industries affected textiles rather later. The Shrewsbury stranglehold on Welsh woollens did not begin to relax till the middle of the eighteenth century. Soon after this some Merioneth manufacturers combined to support a depôt at Barmouth for the direct export of their undressed cloth to the West Indies, where it was much in demand for the clothing of slaves. But the effects of war were disastrous: barely surviving the quarrel with America, the experiment succumbed to the French Wars, leaving it to 'factors' from England to fill the vacuum by buying cloth direct from the loom. Towards the end of the century the woollen trade began to acquire a local organization, with regular markets serving Montgomeryshire for flannel, and Merioneth and the upper Dee valley for rough cloth and hand-knitted stockings. Between them these goods were by this time bringing in nearly £150,000 a year—a mere trifle beside the textile wealth of England, but a welcome supplement to the wages to be earned on the land, especially now that profits were kept at home. Except in the most advanced districts, weaving and spinning were still generally combined with farm work, and the wool was of local growth.

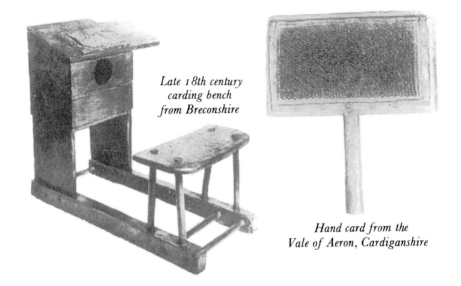

*Late 18th century
carding bench
from Breconshire*

*Hand card from the
Vale of Aeron, Cardiganshire*

Concentration and specialization came with the adoption of machinery for one process after another, and the consequent building of factories. Until nearly the end of the eighteenth century fulling mills, worked by water power, were the only machinery in general use, and their wide distribution is suggested by the frequency of the Welsh equivalent, *pandy*, as a place name. To these the weaver brought his cloth for fulling just as the farmer brought his corn to the grist mill for grinding. The first Welsh textile mill was an offshoot of the Lancashire cotton industry. In 1777 a former partner of Richard Arkwright, who had quarrelled with him, set up on his own by

Fulling mill, Llanrhystud, Cardiganshire, 1835

Woollen mill (Ffatri Fach), Dolgellau, Merioneth

using the water power of Holywell, bringing his labour force with him from Lancashire. Other mills followed, till by 1795 there were well over a thousand operatives. Half of these were women, and three or four hundred 'parish apprentices' brought from Lancashire workhouses were boarded on the spot; there were also two or three hundred outworkers employed at home in neighbouring parishes. For the most part the mills remained alien and ephemeral outposts, with little lasting effect on the life of Wales; all had disappeared before 1870.

About a dozen years after the first cotton mill was set up, factories began to invade the flannel district of Montgomeryshire, and then the cloth districts of Merioneth and Denbighshire; but never the knitting industry at Bala. This remained a handicraft practised widely by women and children who knitted as they walked, 'setting a laudable example to the sluggard and the beggar'. It was between 1800 and 1840 that factories spread most rapidly and most widely. In Merioneth the industry remained essentially rural: there was no wholesale migration of labour, no sudden emergence of a specialized industrial labour force. Much of the early machinery could be made by local craftsmen and installed by people with no education and little capital. Such men were apt to succumb to the crises which beset industry during and after the Napoleonic Wars.

The Montgomeryshire flannel industry was by 1840 employing between two and three thousand textile workers, including a high proportion of women and children. Compared with the Yorkshire industry, where Leeds alone had four times as many operatives as the whole of Montgomeryshire, it was not an impressive growth, but it was bringing a touch of prosperity to the centres of the industry, and creating the nucleus of an urbanized working class. As country industry declined, depriving the small farmer of a subsidiary source of income, manufacture was concentrated at Llanidloes and Newtown, the 'very small market town, not containing more than one thousand inhabitants', with 'no manufactures, except a few flannel looms', which young Robert Owen quitted to seek his fortune in 1781. By 1830 population had grown to 4000. Most of the employers were local men; the operatives overwhelmingly so.

As a centre of industry, however, Montgomeryshire suffered from lack of coal and poor communications. It took thirty years for steam-driven carding machines to invade its factories, and there were only three in 1837; in spinning and in weaving, steam became general only in the second half of the century. But by 1850 the industry had reached its peak, with nearly four thousand workers (about half the total for Wales); in the course of the following decade this shrank by nearly half, and after that decline was rapid.

Expansion in the slate industry of north-western Wales began later and lasted longer; for it did not require new technological inventions but reorganization to meet the rising demand it was uniquely fitted to supply. Early quarrying, like most early mining, was just casual surface-working of the outcrops by small groups armed with pick and shovel. What Humphry Mackworth did for the coal mines of Neath at the end of the

Lord Penrhyn's slate quarry, 1808

seventeenth century, Richard Pennant did nearly a century later for the slate quarries of Penrhyn. Pennant's father, descended from an old Flintshire family, returned from his West Indian sugar plantation with a fortune impressive enough for his son to acquire through marriage, in 1782, the succession to the Penrhyn estate, from which he took the title of Baron Penrhyn. He bought out the many little quarrying partnerships on the estate and took the whole concern into his own hands, installing an efficient manager, and providing adequate roads for land transport and a quay for export, with a tramway to replace the farmers' horses and carts which had served previously. Soon the fifty-four workers had become five hundred. A little later, his neighbour Assheton Smith, lord of the manor of Dinorwic, similarly put a stop to casual quarrying on the waste lands of the manor and developed there an industry second only to Penrhyn.

Parallel developments followed farther south in the Ffestiniog district; but here it was Lancashire prospectors who successfully exploited the property. The workmen, however, were Welsh, almost to a man. Not only was Welsh the language of the quarries, but the workmen often housed themselves in new villages clustering round the Bethesda, Bethel, Carmel or Ebenezer they attended on Sunday, and these Biblical villages, drab and shapeless though they might be, became the home of a vigorous and characteristic Welsh culture.

The Napoleonic Wars imposed a temporary brake on the slate industry but the return of peace meant the return of prosperity. By 1820 employment at Penrhyn had risen tenfold, output twentyfold and profits eightyfold, and North Wales led the world in this branch of production. In 1825 industrial strife made its first appearance at Penrhyn, but the strike, with no organization behind it, was soon broken, and the ringleaders dismissed.

The repeal in 1831 of the duty on the coastwise trade in slates inaugurated half a century of rising prosperity, reaching its peak in the 1880s, when employment had risen to 14,000 — almost twice as many as in the coal mines farther east. This was achieved despite the growing cost of winning the slate, but rising costs were offset by Madocks's new harbour at Portmadoc: linked by a narrow-gauge line with a wide inland quarrying area, this became the main depôt for the export of North Wales slates. At Penrhyn the increasing use of writing slates in schools gave a further burst of prosperity. By mid-century slate-quarrying was becoming the mainstay of both the economy and the folk culture of North Wales.

All these developments called for substantial improvements in transport. At any time before the middle of the eighteenth century 'a Welsh journey' was a byword. Gentlemen naturally went on horseback; the family coach was still restricted to short journeys in level country. Even on horseback a gentleman could be deterred in the mountainous north (as one grumbled in 1721) by 'deluges, tides, rocks and precipices'; and over thirty years later a South Wales gentleman found the 'exceeding bad' state of the roads an obstacle to fixing a date for his mother's burial at a village outside Swansea, only fifty miles away. Loads like iron ore or woollen wares travelled to port or market on pack-mules or ponies.

Pack mules, Merthyr to Cardiff, 1794

The only through routes on which any care was expended, above the parochial 'statute labour' of villagers under an un-trained surveyor, were those leading to Ireland; for important officials and urgent mails might be concerned. On the 'Irish' road leading to Holyhead, recurrent attempts were made to mitigate for travellers the terrors of Penmaenmawr, that sheer precipice 'over which', a Stuart topographer declared, 'yf either man or beaste shoulde fall, both sea and rocke . . . woulde strive and contend whether of bothe should doe hym the greatest mischief'. Roads leading to Fishguard or Milford were not seriously tackled till after the Napoleonic Wars. Otherwise wheeled traffic was confined to the lumbering farmer's wain, and in the more mountainous regions even this had to give place to the wheel-less *car llusg* or the sledge.

From mid-century agricultural societies were turning their attention to the roads, notably the pioneer society of Brecon-shire. Soon after its inception in 1755 this enterprising body contrived to jog into activity some of the parishes lying on the post road from Herefordshire to west Wales. It also encouraged road-building near mines and lime kilns, and the county set an example by appointing a paid surveyor for all its roads. In the following decade Anthony Bacon got his farming neighbours to join him in improving the tracks over which their produce had to travel between Merthyr and Cardiff, and other mine-owners and iron-masters followed his lead.

The bridging of the many rivers owed much to that inspired amateur William Edwards, a farmer and Dissenting minister who after building his own chapel turned his hand to more ambitious schemes. Between 1746 and 1754 he succeeded, at the fourth costly attempt, in throwing a single-span bridge across the Tâf, where the industrial town of Pontypridd later sprang up. Both mechanically and aesthetically it was one of the wonders of its day. Edwards and his three sons were also responsible for more than a dozen other bridges in South Wales.

In the second half of the century the construction of roads and bridges became a collective rather than an individual enterprise. During the next seventy or eighty years turnpike trusts were set up by successive Acts of Parliament, which

The last of the turnpike gates, (Llanfairpwll, Anglesey), c, 1895

CARDIFF & LONDON

In One Day!!!

The Public are respectfully informed, a new and elegant Fast Four-horse Coach

'ST. DAVID!'

LEAVES THE

ANGEL INN,

CARDIFF, every

TUESDAY, THURSDAY, & SATURDAY MORNING,

AT SIX O'CLOCK;

NEWPORT,	- at a Quarter past	**7**;
CHEPSTOW,	- -	**9**;
NEWNHAM,	- -	**11**;
GLOUCESTER,	Half-past	**12**;
AND **CHELTENHAM,**	Half-past	**1**;

AND ARRIVES IN

LONDON at **9** o'clock the same Evening.

BRADLEY & Co., Proprietors.

On the arrival of this Coach at CHELTENHAM, the Railway Train starts for **Worcester, Birmingham,** and all Parts of the North; and returns from Cheltenham, MONDAYS, WEDNESDAYS, and FRIDAYS, at Half-past **12**, after the arrival of the Railway Trains from Birmingham, &c.

W. PAINE, PRINTER 127, HIGH STREET, CHELTENHAM

Coaching poster, Cardiff, 1840

empowered them to levy tolls to meet their costs. Starting on the borders, they spread gradually westward until about a fifth of the road surface of Wales was under their control. Some of them appointed paid surveyors, some even consulted James Loudon Macadam about surfacing, and professional standards began to replace the farce of statute labour, although this remained legally enforceable till the General Highways Act of 1835—with the unhappy result that country roads not covered by a trust tended to be more neglected than ever.

On the more frequented roads the turnpikes brought in the age of the stage coach and the stage wagon. A stage coach was running from Brecon to London by 1757, but it took another twenty years for long-distance public transport to reach the more rugged parts of North Wales. The adoption of this conveyance for the royal mails stimulated coaching everywhere, especially on the Irish mail routes. Mail coaches were put on the road to Holyhead from Chester (later Shrewsbury), and from Brecon to Milford. After the Union with Ireland in 1800 the road from London to Holyhead became the subject of a parliamentary inquiry, which resulted in the first exchequer grant for the roads after the Napoleonic Wars were over. Thomas Telford, the leading road engineer of his day, was in charge of the work, which brought two major roads to North Wales (one inland from Shrewsbury, the other following the coast from Chester), and two superb suspension bridges spanning respectively the Conwy and the Menai Strait.

Unfortunately, no important Welsh industry gained much from this great undertaking. But by stimulating road improvement everywhere it brought about a revolution in social life. Soon all the main roads were aswarm with coaches, 'fly wagons' and post chaises, and even people below the rank of 'carriage folk' could depend on regular transport and postal deliveries.

For the industries of South Wales canals were probably more important than the turnpikes. Canals provided quicker and smoother carriage than the roads to the coast for the products of the industrial area centred on Merthyr. North Wales was less fortunate. Its principal canals were constructed soon after those of the south but, while of benefit to farming, they were of relatively little help to industry. The Ellesmere canal, as projected in 1795, would have afforded outlets for the coal and

125

Pontcysyllte aqueduct

iron of east Denbighshire at Chester and at Ellesmere Port on the Mersey; but the terrain enforced a route which served no important industry. Work on the Montgomeryshire canal was interrupted by the war, and it did not reach Newtown till 1819, a time of severe slump in the woollen industry.

The railway age in Wales began with the inclines, levels and tramways that were built to provide smooth passage for breakable goods like coal and slate. Before the end of the seventeenth century Mackworth had laid down wooden rails at his Neath collieries; after 1750 they became common in most of the mining and quarrying districts, and were sometimes rivals to the canals.

Then came steam locomotion. In 1804 Trevithick's engine hauled a ten-ton load and seventy passengers from the ironworks at Pen y darren to the Glamorgan canal. This invention proved a flash in the pan, but iron railroads continued to proliferate until by 1811 the South Wales coal field alone had nearly 150 miles of them. The first railway in Wales operated by steam locomotive was the Taff Vale, built in 1841 by Isambard Brunel (and largely financed by the Guests of Dowlais) to link Merthyr with Cardiff. Between then and mid-century the more westerly industrial regions were linked with Swansea and Llanelli. At the same time Brunel engineered the trunk line connecting Swansea and Cardiff with Newport and Chepstow, then extended it to join the Great Western system and so to establish railway communication with London.

The main expansion of railways in South Wales was yet to come, but already the effects were felt in the iron industry, which provided rails for so many of them. Even more important were the effects on Cardiff. Up to the end of the eighteenth century, the future capital was a small market town of under two thousand inhabitants, and primarily an exporter of agricultural produce. The output of the industrial expansion of the 1760s flowed mainly into Swansea and Newport, but from 1830 exploitation of the northern coal measures, developed in the first place to meet the needs of the heavy industries, was yielding a surplus of a quality that enabled it to compete with the north of England in the London market, and in the following decade, after the removal of export duties, to begin nearly a century's domination of the French market.

By 1839 the coal brought to Cardiff by canal was more than the quay could cope with, and new docks built by the marquess of Bute came just in time to accommodate the extra loads brought by the railway, as well as the increasing tonnage of shipping that bore them abroad. Cardiff's population grew more than sixfold by 1830 and by mid-century nearly tenfold. Greater things lay ahead, but Cardiff's prosperity was firmly founded in the thirties and forties.

It was a different story in North Wales. The claims of the Irish traffic took precedence over internal communications, and the costly route chosen for it by Robert Stephenson in 1846 by-passed the chief regional industries in favour of a line (as a rival protested), 'bounded by the sea on one hand and by almost inaccessible hills on the other, having no . . . means of connection but with the places it may actually pass'. It involved yet another crossing of the Straits, this time by the novel expedient of a tubular bridge. But along this coastal strip the railway did much to develop the seasonal (though precarious) industry of catering for summer visitors. The

Climbing Cader Idris, 1814

resorts of Cardigan Bay and the south-west had to make do
with the stage coach for another decade and more; but long
before this, the age of romanticism had brought into the
remoter highlands travellers on horseback or afoot, un-
deterred by the 'Welsh ways over the mountains' which
Charles I's men had found such a sore trial. The spate of
English 'tours in Wales' from 1770 onwards amounted to the
discovery of an unknown land.

On the other hand, the railway from Chester to Shrewsbury,
built about the same time as the coastal line to Holyhead,
passed through the mineral district of east Denbighshire, with
a short branch linking it with some of the colliery tramways.
It was soon absorbed into the Great Western system, giving
access through Chester to the north coast and to London and
South Wales. But by then the halcyon days of the north-eastern
iron industry were over, and local coal resources were insuffi-

cient to compete in wider markets. In fact it was during the early railway age that the pattern emerged of the south-east as primarily urban and industrial, while the north and west retained a predominantly rural character.

In terms of population 'rural Wales' still meant three-quarters of the country even after the upheavals of the Napoleonic period, and two-thirds as late as 1850; in terms of area, of course, much more. And rural Wales was relatively unchanging, apart from the social impact of Methodism and the hardships brought about by war and enclosure. In Stuart days Monmouthshire was the only Welsh county where the Elizabethan Poor Law operated fully because although many lived well below the 'poverty line', this was accepted as normal, while church collections and the bounty of the Hall could generally cope with famine or pestilence. In many sparsely-populated Welsh parishes it was only after 1775 that poor rates were first collected, and not till the Napoleonic Wars did their catastrophic increase begin to arouse general alarm. Lax administration of the Poor Law before 1834 was blamed for improvident marriages and families too big, even allowing for infant mortality, to be supported without parish relief.

Some of the excess was siphoned off by emigration to the United States. In colonial days emigration had been predominantly a religious adventure; in the late eighteenth and early nineteenth centuries it became a flight from intolerable economic conditions. Yet the ideological motive lingered on, notably in the migration to Cambria settlement in western Pennsylvania, planned by the Baptist minister Morgan J. Rhees, as the home of a 'free and enlightened people when the old Cambria is neglected and despised'. Conservative opinion, however, whether Anglican or Methodist, long remained hostile to emigration.

In any case it only touched the fringe of rural poverty. Many could not afford it; many looked for relief in industry; but mostly the Welsh peasant clung to his meagre holding. Up to 1840 there was no general flight from the countryside, where population went on growing with each successive census. It was not until the second half of the century that the railway covered enough of the country to flood village shops with

English manufactures and to drive a nail in the coffin of rural handicrafts. The peasant's life had always been hard; the Industrial Revolution, while adding new hardships, also made escape easier, and so began the process of rural disintegration.

The real revolution was in the industrial areas, and it was still far from complete in mid-century. The only urban aggregation in Wales that could compare with English industrial centres was Merthyr. There, what was called 'the village'— where the shopkeeping and professional classes lived—was largely run by the same families as in the days of rural seclusion. On the outskirts lived 'the inhabitants of the ironworks', an amorphous population which grew more and more mixed in origin as the catchment area widened. Here government lay in the hands of the Guests, whose 'tommy shop' supplied the needs of the inhabitants and kept them distinct from the 'village'. The works bounded their whole horizon; and the speed of industrial growth produced living conditions which were a by-word throughout Wales. On the south coast devastation went even deeper, since the copper fumes wrought irreparable damage to the very vegetation.

In the northern counties everything was on a smaller scale. Only in the limited area of Parys Mountain did copper smelting bring about anything like the havoc of the Swansea Bay belt, and in the north-eastern coalfield the nearest approach to Merthyr was the overgrown village of Rhos Llanerchrugog, which had sprouted on empty moorland to accommodate a population of some five thousand, in conditions described in a government report as 'worse than Merthyr Tydvil'. On the other hand, the immigrants were drawn, as those of Merthyr originally were, almost exclusively from the adjacent countryside, and Rhos remained a village in spirit, with an inner coherence and a lively culture of its own. The flannel towns of Montgomeryshire were different again, for they were ancient market towns never completely swamped by the factory population, and textile handicrafts had long been firmly rooted in the surrounding villages and farms; what was new was the factory, and that was incompletely mechanized. At Holywell, the centre of the short-lived cotton industry and the copper and brass industries, the works flanked a watercourse outside the bounds of the town. And the mushrooming quarrying villages remained essentially rural in tone.

The major developments had all taken place since 1780, and one of their most striking effects had been the emergence of a distinct industrial working class. This was not achieved without the friction that accompanied the transition everywhere: to the enclosure riots of the early nineteenth century and the food riots of the eighteenth were now added, especially after 1815, sporadic industrial strikes. So far they had no organization behind them; trade unionism took no lasting root till the second half of the century, but from about 1830 we begin to trace the lineaments of a conscious working-class movement.

Further Reading

W. Rees, *Industry before the Industrial Revolution* (2 vols.), 1968.

A. H. Dodd, *The Industrial Revolution in North Wales*, 3rd ed., 1971.

A. H. John, *The Industrial Development of South Wales*, 1950.

W. E. Minchinton (ed.), *Industrial South Wales, 1750–1914*, 1969.

R. O. Roberts, 'The development and decline of the copper and other non-ferrous industries in South Wales', *Transactions of Hon. Society of Cymmrodorion*, 1956.

D. Dylan Pritchard, 'The expansionist phase in the history of the Welsh slate industry', *Transactions of Caernarvonshire Hist. Soc.*, 1959.

Geraint Jenkins, *The Welsh Woollen Industry*, 1969.

J. Rowland, *Copper Mountain*, 1965.

J. P. Addis, *The Crawshay Dynasty*, 1957.

VII

Towards Contemporary Wales
1780–1914

By the middle of the nineteenth century most of the characteristic features of Wales as it appeared before the two World
Wars, had taken shape. The broad lines of division between
industrial and rural Wales had already been sketched out: in
the ensuing years the first grew at the expense of the second,
with far-reaching social consequences. The new industrial
working class had begun to make its presence felt by the time
of Waterloo, but it took another fifty years to achieve an
effective organization, and then only in a limited number of
industries; long before this the sporadic unrest of the early
years had come to a head in industrial Wales in two Chartist
outbreaks and in rural Wales in the Rebecca riots. In religion
the revival which began in the 1730s had for the following
fifty years little impact on the north; but from then on both
north and south experienced profound changes in popular
religion, and in social habits fostered by it. By the middle of
the nineteenth century this transformation reached a climax,
and old landmarks were being steadily eroded.

Alongside this went the revival of pride in national culture
of which the Cymmrodorion Society had been the herald. The
movement grew to maturity in the atmosphere of romanticism
which marked the closing years of the century and found
expression in the resuscitated eisteddfod. Among the Welsh
community in London, romanticism was allied with the radical
sentiments of the American and French Revolutions; but in
Wales itself such sentiments were strongly condemned by

Methodist leaders until after 1850, and only found support in more heterodox religious circles, mainly in South Wales. Out of the fusion of these elements— religious, political, cultural and economic— emerged the Wales of the late nineteenth and early twentieth centuries.

By 1780, the Methodist movement had spread widely in the southern counties, but in the north it was confined to a few centres, largely dependent on leadership from the south. A new chapter was opened in 1784 by the settlement at Bala of

Field preaching, Anglesey, early 19th century

Thomas Charles, an ordained but unbeneficed Anglican parson with zeal and organizing ability, who soon made Bala the centre of North Wales Methodism. From here missions penetrated regions hitherto untouched, and soon after the Napoleonic War Methodism swept the new quarrying areas and the heart of Snowdonia in a succession of revivals which kept groups of villages at fever heat for weeks on end.

The older Dissenting denominations, never strong in Wales, were at first inclined to look askance at this renewed onset of field preaching; but by the end of the eighteenth century they, too, were infected by the new 'enthusiasm', and from early in the nineteenth there set in a fever of chapel-building— by the Methodists as an adjunct to, and by the old Dissenters as a substitute for, the parish church. These early chapels, often built at great personal sacrifice by the worshippers, naturally followed the lines of the makeshift accommodation they replaced; only as congregations grew in size, wealth and in-

An early Nonconformist chapel (Capel Newydd, Llangian, Caernarvonshire),
built 1769

fluence were more elaborate and fashionable structures
attempted. They added a characteristic feature to the landscape. Under the Toleration Act they had to be licensed as
'places of worship for Protestant Dissenters'; such licences
became common from the closing decades of the eighteenth
century.

Interior of Capel Newydd

The Methodists were in a difficult position because of their disinclination to brand themselves as 'Dissenters'; yet without doing so they were liable to prosecution for worshipping in unlicensed premises—as they found when the panic caused by the French Revolution made all abnormal assemblies suspect and open to visitations by disorderly mobs or by officers of the law. Towards the end of the eighteenth century, advised by Thomas Charles, they began licensing their chapels, and so took a first step towards becoming a Dissenting sect. The final step was taken when in 1811 Charles conferred on eight lay preachers what were in effect Presbyterian orders. From then till the middle of the century the new denomination grew rapidly, but it still held itself aloof from the older sects, especially in politics. After 1850 the old and new Nonconformity combined to give a distinctive colour to the whole religious, moral and political life of Wales. An attempt to include in the census of 1851 statistics of religious affiliations led to the conclusion that some eighty per cent of the Welsh people rated themselves as members or, more vaguely, 'adherents' of Nonconformist bodies; and this before the revival of 1859 increased the total by an estimated eighty thousand.

Holyhead Wakes

It is a commonplace that the religious revivals took out of the country's life much of its carefree joyousness, and killed many old customs and traditions. The *gwylmabsantau* or Wakes, which like the *pardon* in Brittany or the *mardi gras* in New Orleans had combined traditional religion with licensed roistering, withered under the onslaughts of the preachers; so did the *anterliwt*, or folk drama, which had degenerated in both form and content and was reprobated by men of culture who were not Methodists. It was inevitably the middle classes who took the lead in the new religious movements, and it was natural that they should inculcate the middle-class virtues of sobriety, thrift and deference to authority; contemporary social commentators all emphasize these as fruits of the revivals. But fairs and markets, though less boisterous, did not cease to be important social occasions—notably those of Carmarthen or Wrexham. The preachers inveighed from the start against excessive drinking, but teetotalism, a word and a principle originating in Lancashire in the 1830s, did not capture Welsh Nonconformity until the following decade.

Meanwhile the Church in Wales was beginning to set her own house in order and to recover the ground lost by the

Carmarthen market in early Victorian times

Methodist secession and the resurgence of the older Non-conformity. It began in the early years of the century with the measures taken by Bishop Burgess of St David's for improving the education of his clergy. These culminated in the foundation in 1822 of Lampeter College, which helped materially to raise clerical standards through the whole country. There followed a readjustment of parish boundaries to meet the needs of a shifting population, extensive rebuilding or restoration of existing churches and parsonages and the addition of new ones, and the removal of hoary abuses like pluralism.

The claims of the Welsh language—a great source of strength to Methodism—were fully recognized by Bishop Burgess, Englishman though he was (like all his brother bishops in Wales till 1870); but the strength of the Welsh revival in Church life lay in Bangor diocese, whose parish clergy made substantial contributions to the literary and antiquarian movement, with encouragement from English-speaking bishops and deans. Many of them were also actively promoting the Tractarian movement, which by restoring some of the ritual discarded at the Reformation, and exalting the 'priestly' character of the clergy, roused Protestant suspicions. Strong resentment was felt among old-fashioned parishioners, often including the squire, who found himself relegated to a secondary position in what he had come to regard as his own domain. But the rift within the Church was as nothing to the widening gulf between Church and Chapel. Methodists, always a bulwark of Protestantism and fiercely opposed to Catholic Emancipation, drew closer to the older Nonconformity, which reacted towards ritualism as it had in the days of Laud.

These fears were deepened by the influx from Catholic Ireland into the 'ironworks' belt of north Glamorgan and north Monmouthshire and into the 'resort' area of North Wales, and from Catholic Lancashire into the north-eastern coalfield. At the beginning of the nineteenth century the Roman Catholic population of Wales was about a thousand families, served from eight mission centres. A diminishing number had clung to their ancestral faith in places like Holywell in the north-east and Abergavenny, Chepstow and Usk in the south-east. Occasional missions were organized from these centres, or from across the border, or by religious orders on the continent, but before 1829 public worship was illegal. The Welsh Catholic community was too insignificant to have its own organization until a Welsh district was formed in 1840 and full diocesan organization in the following decade; but the building of churches and the settlement of resident priests checked the drift of Catholic immigrants into Protestantism or mere indifference.

By the middle of the century the adherents of Rome had multiplied tenfold; but they were still mainly Irish. In industrial South Wales they tended to be a reservoir of cheap blackleg labour, and so to provoke many a bloody fray; in the north this aspect was less important, but religious prejudice remained strong. The intention of an immigrant Lancashire ironmaster to build a church for his co-religionists at Wrexham had to be concealed from the owner of the land; and at Caernarvon as late as 1866 a threatening mob had to be headed off a building destined for Catholic worship. Not till after 1850 was there any substantial number of conversions among the native Welsh, or a priesthood able to evangelize them in their own tongue.

Eighteenth-century politics in Wales, as in most of England, amounted to little more than a gentlemanly game of cricket, with exclusive family groups at the wicket, their dependants in the outfield, and glittering trophies for the champions. Only at rare intervals did more vital issues obtrude themselves. The ebbing of the panic caused by the French Revolution, together with the growth of Dissent and the rise of new social groups, brought about a new political climate. By 1830 the agitation for parliamentary reform had begun to capture the growing middle class, especially in industrial Wales. At the same time there was acute distress among industrial workmen; poor rates soared, and more than once the militia had to quell incipient riots. Towards the end of the year delegates from Lancashire appeared in the Denbighshire and Flintshire coalfield to recruit for their newly-formed trade union. After many stormy passages, the owners promised to remedy some grievances; an uneasy peace was restored, and a sympathetic bench dealt leniently with the rioters. But trade remained bad, and although discontent still rumbled through the coalfield, the union petered out within a year.

The following summer the Lancashire agitators extended their operations to Merthyr, bearing funds raised by North Wales groups. But here the situation was far more complex. Hitherto the mixed population of 'the ironworks' had followed the middle-class leadership of 'the village'; but miners and ironworkers had their own class grievances, which had led to widespread but sporadic outbreaks—not without bloodshed and barricades—ever since the war ended. Following a heavy cut in wages announced at Cyfarthfa, the 'inhabitants of the ironworks' swarmed into Merthyr to demonstrate against the 'shopocracy', whose appeal brought in both militia and regulars. A pitched battle ensued, with nearly a hundred casualties, including twenty killed; there followed the public execution of the young coalminer Richard Lewis ('Dic Penderyn'), on a charge of wounding a soldier. He became a popular martyr, and when the Lancashire emissaries appeared, their persuasions induced a wave of strikes and lockouts, in which the union fared no better than in the north-east. The onset of cholera caused a further depression of spirits, and with the resumption of the struggle for parliamentary reform the 'shopocracy' returned to power. The Reform Act of 1832 made Merthyr a parliamentary borough, and the middle-class electorate of 580 returned as its first member J. J. Guest the ironmaster, who retained the seat for the rest of his life.

The Reform Act gave civic pride to Merthyr ; elsewhere there was speedy disillusionment. Among the firstfruits were the workhouses built under the Poor Law of 1834. In Montgomeryshire this coincided with a slump in the woollen industry causing widespread distress among the weavers—a responsible and hitherto prosperous body of workers whose anger became focused on the grim 'prisons' which awaited them if they fell on the rates. In such an atmosphere Chartism, with its promise of political reform, readily took root. Local branches were formed, from which delegates were sent to the Chartist conventions in London; local demonstrations were held, and preparations made for armed resistance should

Chartist affray at Newport, 1839

'moral force' fail to secure the Charter. The following spring
the authorities drafted in police reinforcements, including
three of the new London 'peelers'. Their arrival in Llanidloes
touched off a riot in which prisoners were rescued, the police
beaten up and their quarters sacked. For four days the
Chartists were in control; but shops and factories went on
working and the Chartists maintained order in the town until
the military arrived. Then arrests were made and three of the
ringleaders were condemned to transportation.

Chartism had meanwhile been spreading in rural west Wales and the industrial south-east. Here too the leadership was in the hands of middle-class radicals of Nonconformist background, most of them averse to physical force. By 1839 nearly thirty thousand signatures had been procured for the Chartist petition, over half of them from Merthyr, where the 'moral force' party now prevailed. The centre of militancy was in industrial Monmouthshire, where the popular English Chartist leader Henry Vincent lay in prison. This was the region which had been terrorized by periodic raids from gangs of lowing

'Scotch cattle', under a leader wearing bull's horns, bent on wreaking vengeance on suspected blacklegs or informers. On a soaking autumn night in 1839 three columns converged on Newport with no very clear plans except another mammoth demonstration. Inevitably there was a scuffle with the soldiers stationed there to meet any insurrection, and the three leaders (including John Frost, a well-to-do draper who had been mayor of the borough) were arrested and eventually transported.

Chartism lingered on in South Wales till 1848, but it was never again a formidable force. In the north-eastern coalfield and in Snowdonia it never took root at all. In both areas Calvinistic Methodism, which had set its face against trade unions and political agitation, was strong, and Unitarianism, with its bent towards subversive politics, virtually non-existent. In other respects the two areas differed, the one plunged in deep depression by the decline of the local iron industry, the other buoyed up by the Whig government's repeal of the slate duty.

Political radicalism of a milder hue found a congenial home among the older Nonconformist bodies; indeed the chapel provided the only means of collective political expression for those outside the narrow circle of the electorate, and the denominational press which began to proliferate from 1830 was a powerful factor in their political education. But these were still a middle-class *elite*: the rank and file clung to their traditional (and prudent) allegiance to the gentry who were their employers or their landlords—or both.

In rural west Wales the grievances expressed in Chartism, sharpened by the bad harvest of 1838, found a new target in turnpike gates, the visible symbol of the small farmer's burdens —for tolls were especially frequent and troublesome here. Gangs of men, many in female disguise, ranged the country at night, seeking out their quarry and evading capture with the skill of a guerilla army. Their leaders went under the name of 'Rebecca', claiming the blessing pronounced on her scriptural namesake, 'let thy seed possess the gate of those which hate them'. Troops were called in, and several of the ringleaders were sentenced to transportation; but a commission of inquiry in 1844 resulted in legislation which removed many of the turnpike grievances.

By this time emissaries of the Anti-Corn Law League, encouraged by the Nonconformist press and pulpit, were persuading peasant and artisan that their grievances hinged on laws which bolstered the price of corn, bringing no benefit except to the anglicized landlord. In 1843 over a thousand miners from Rhos Llanerchrugog, which had eschewed Chartism, signed an appeal to Queen Victoria placing on the Corn Laws the responsibility for their desperate plight.

Hardly had the Corn Law controversy been settled by Repeal in 1846 when a new issue arose, further widening the gap between Church and Chapel. The report of the Rebecca commission had raised the question English Puritans had posed two centuries earlier; whether 'the more speedie attaining of our English tongue' was not the only way to rescue the Welsh people from barbarism. But now the concern was less with their 'exceeding ignorance of our holy God and of all true and good learning' than with the threat to law and order exhibited by the Monmouthshire Chartists and by Rebecca. Many Welsh parents shared these doubts: they were concerned at

Satire on Education investigators, 1847

the handicaps suffered by a monoglot Welsh child in industry and the professions. It was a Welsh businessman representing an English constituency who in 1846 procured the appointment of an inquiry into the state of education in Wales, 'especially into the means afforded to the labouring classes of acquiring a knowledge of English'.

Their report was published in the following year, and caused a tremendous stir. As a statistical review of Welsh education it is invaluable; its revelations administered a salutary shock, for education was in a deplorable backwater. The grammar school endowments had completely failed to keep pace with needs, and their masters could make a livelihood only by encouraging fee-paying pupils at the expense of the 'free scholars' for whom they had been founded; their part in the educational life of the country amounted to little. At the elementary level, the Circulating schools had undoubtedly widened the range of literacy, but for almost thirty years after 'Madam' Bevan's death in 1779 her endowment for their continuance lay in chancery, and the work was held up.

Many attempts were made by private individuals to fill the gap, but these were naturally sporadic. There were numerous small parish legacies for teaching poor children to read, but these only provided for the handful who could be taught in the vestry or a church pew, and their effectiveness depended on the energy of the incumbent, curate or parish clerk. And there were many ephemeral 'private adventure' schools, ranging from the expensive 'academy for sons of gentlemen' to the humbler 'dame school' charging only a few pence; some were conducted by dedicated spirits who made a real impact, some by the 'throw-outs' of society. None had any permanent buildings, staff or endowment; all depended on individuals who came and went.

The educational drive initiated in the early nineteenth century by the two great voluntary societies, and from 1833 meagrely subsidized by the state, had so far affected Wales only marginally. The undenominational British Society had little appeal for Anglican landlords, who were best placed for providing the sites and the financial guarantees, and it was only after an appeal in 1843 from a London Welshman, Hugh

Owen, that schools of this type began to spread in Wales. On the other hand, Nonconformist parents were reluctant to send their children to schools of the National Society, where the atmosphere was exclusively Anglican, and this meant wide areas where the children had no schooling at all. Where they had, the teachers' qualifications left much to be desired; drawn from the ranks of impoverished weavers or small farmers for whom a guaranteed salary of £25 to £35 a year was a fortune, they were often intelligent men with a taste for reading, but their training rarely amounted to more than a few weeks at a 'model school'. Training colleges did not appear in Wales until the second half of the century. Most serious of all, the teaching was in a language only half understood by the pupils and often far from familiar to the teachers.

This was a fundamental problem on which the government investigators were ill-fitted to pronounce; unhappily they reported with a confidence which impelled an Anglican critic to quote at them the Book of Ecclesiasticus: 'First understand, and then rebuke', and which branded their report as *Brad y Llyfrau Gleision*—'the Treachery of the Blue Books'. Obsessed by their terms of reference, the commissioners equated literacy with facility in English, and interpreted as crass ignorance inability to answer questions rapped out in an unfamiliar tongue and accent. Their conviction that the two basic evils of Welsh life were the persistence of the language and the dominance of Dissent furbished up new weapons for political Nonconformity and linked it more closely to nationalist sentiment; this was true even of the Methodists, who had hitherto looked askance at the heterodox tendencies they associated with the London sponsors of the eisteddfod.

On the other hand, the Methodists were among the staunchest supporters of the Sunday School, an institution borrowed from England but given a Welsh dress by the admission of adult pupils, and the systematic teaching of the Welsh language as a basis for Scripture study in the mother tongue. It thus became an important adjunct to the national revival. Even the government commissioners praised this institution; but they naturally knew nothing of the Welsh literary and antiquarian renaissance that had been flourishing for half a century, finding expression in a brisk output of new poetry and the printing of Welsh classics hitherto available only in manuscript.

Up to this point, Welsh national consciousness had been focused mainly on culture; but from 1843 the propaganda of the Liberation Society, which stood for the separation of Church and State, brought an infusion of politics. In England 'Liberationism' was part of advanced liberal theory, with no immediate practical application; in Wales the traditional prejudice was less against religious establishments as such than against the domination of Canterbury over the Welsh Church. During the next quarter-century the assiduous campaigning of Henry Richard, a Welsh minister who abandoned his London pastorate for the secretaryship of the Peace Society, bore fruit in the formation of over fifty 'Liberationist' branches, providing local pressure-groups round which any political agitation could crystallize.

Pressure-groups could achieve little without the vote, and the spread of the Liberation Society came just in time for Disraeli's extension in 1867 of the franchise to social grades where Nonconformity was strong. The memorable election in 1868 gave a new face to Welsh politics. In nearly two-thirds of the constituencies traditional leaders were overthrown by newcomers of Liberal and Nonconformist leanings; the political habits of two centuries had been thrown off. Not that there was any significant change in the social group from which members were drawn; what was significant was the large number of evictions of tenants who dared to break loose politically from their landlords—as many as seventy in Cardigan and Carmarthen; a sure sign of waning self-confidence among the country's historic leaders.

The 1868 election brought Gladstone to power. It also brought Welsh Nonconformity into the House of Commons. The story of the evictions lost nothing in the telling, and led directly to Gladstone's Ballot Act of 1872. In Wales the evictions brought the land question to the forefront, with its overtones of religion and nationalism: an Anglican, English-speaking gentry on one side, a Nonconformist, Welsh-speaking tenantry on the other. All this gave political direction to the long agricultural depression and the drain into industry of the younger element in the rural population. Planned migrations, again mostly under Nonconformist leadership, to establish a Welsh settlement across the Atlantic were again attempted; one of them, in unsettled lands in Patagonia, precariously survived, to celebrate its centenary a few years ago.

In industrial Wales the outstanding features of the closing decades of the century were the continuing decline of the northern industries and expansion of the southern ones, the growing dependence of the latter on coal exports, the growth of Cardiff and Swansea, and the rise of trade unionism The textile industry of mid-Wales shrank to a shadow of its former self; a brief revival of lead mining in the 1870s succumbed to foreign competition within twenty years. The heavy industries of the north-east languished except for the establishment at Brymbo of open-hearth steel manufacture in 1884 and the industrial development of Deeside in the following decade. Slate quarrying remained in full vigour until foreign competition and industrial strife began to take their toll in the 1880s.

It was in South Wales that the most spectacular developments were seen. Coal, instead of playing second fiddle to iron, came to dominate the economy: when Thomas Powell, who had pioneered the trade to France, died in 1863, he was the greatest coal exporter in the world. Production had spread to the Rhondda valleys, whose incomparable steam coal lay so deep that it had been deemed unworkable. The first train load of Rhondda coal entered Cardiff in 1855; ten years later David Davies, a Montgomeryshire farmer climbing to fortune as a railway contractor, risked his capital in pits of unprecedented depth, and soon the valleys were transformed into a human warren with twenty-four thousand souls to the square mile.

The transition from sail to steam in the course of the 1860s added a new home demand, for the steamship companies early found that Welsh coal best suited their needs, and by 1885 the Admiralty was using it exclusively. No wonder that the population of Cardiff grew tenfold in sixty years, and her annual coal exports from under a million to ten million tons. A few miles away, at the tiny hamlet of Barry, David Davies

Rhondda before industrialisation

Rhondda after industrialisation (aerial photograph)

had a new dock made and connected with his coal mines. When it was completed in 1889 the population of Barry rose from under 100 to 1,300, and in 1911 it created a record by shipping eleven million tons of coal. The deepening mines were a source of frequent disaster, whether from explosions (despite the fact that it was here that the Davy lamp first came into its own), or from the more frequent roof-falls. To posterity they left the legacy brought home by the tragedy of Aberfan.

Coal was king, but iron, tinplate and copper stood near the throne. Increasing dependence on foreign ores drew the iron industry to the coast, and Cardiff replaced Merthyr, leaving a trail of derelict sites, till at last, in 1891, the Dowlais works moved to near Cardiff. At the same time the transition from iron to steel increased the scale and cost of production, and weeded out the smaller concerns. Copper and tinplate had always clung to the coast because of their ancient Cornish connections, and the substitution of ores from abroad involved no extensive displacement. By 1875 the tinplate industry of Swansea almost monopolized this branch of trade till the McKinley tariff of 1891 drove it out of the American market, where it had been the chief supplier of the canning industry; but by the First World War new markets had been found, and production was brisker than ever. Copper smelting had reached its peak by 1890, after which it was overwhelmed by foreign competition, but Swansea had meanwhile grown into a great port, second only to Cardiff in population, and all set to accommodate new industries like nickel production.

The new capitalists borne to fortune on the boom in the coal industry were mostly Welsh countrymen with strong Nonconformist backgrounds; so were the miners who benefited from what, to the Welsh farm worker, were dazzlingly high wages. Both carried their rural habits of mind into the newly industrialized valleys and it has been suggested that the chief link between rural and industrial Wales was the chapel, which loomed so large in the life of both. During the 1870s trade unions began to acquire a firm footing in the principal industries, and were now throwing up their own leaders, instead of depending on outside initiative. The North Wales quarrymen were organized by W. J. Parry, a quarryman's son who had raised himself to a comfortable professional standing; the South Wales miners by a former door-boy named William Abraham, but better known in bardic circles as Mabon. Both were ardent Welshmen, Liberals and Nonconformists. Under their leadership both industries, after bitter initial struggles, arrived at a *modus vivendi* between employers and employed which lasted till nearly the end of the century.

By 1911 the population had nearly reached two and a half million, instead of a little over a million in 1851; but five-eighths of this total was concentrated in the two south-eastern shires, and two out of every three Welshmen were town dwellers. It was no longer true, moreover, that this increase was predominantly drawn from Welsh-speaking Wales: half the inhabitants of Glamorgan were already English monoglots in 1891, and during the first decade of the new century the influx of nearly 130,000 into the coalfield came mainly from England. This new situation produced two contradictory effects. On the one hand those who treasured the Welsh language and traditional Welsh values clung to them more self-consciously. The eisteddfod had become a popular annual event instead of an esoteric cult. In 1856 a Pontypridd weaver and his son composed *Hen Wlad fy Nhadau*, and its popularity soon gave it the standing of a national anthem. But it grew increasingly clear that advancement depended on fluency in English; so despite the furore over the Blue Books, the attitude they expressed was widely held by ambitious Welsh parents.

This threat to the mother tongue brought into being in the last two decades of the century a succession of patriotic societies designed to bolster it up, and the controversy began to colour Welsh politics. Gladstone, an avowed believer in Welsh nationhood by 1880, became a hero of Welsh Nonconformity, whose portrait shared farmhouse and cottage walls with those of eminent Welsh preachers and politicians and foreign nationalist idols like Mazzini and Garibaldi. Welsh leaders began to discover similarities between their plight and that of their Irish cousins, who were occupying so much of Gladstone's attention. His disestablishment of the Irish Church was an object lesson, and his extension of the franchise in 1884, nearly trebling the Welsh rural vote, gave a preponderance to the nationalist, Nonconformist element in Welsh Liberalism, which intensified the demand for disestablishment.

This had its material as well as its more idealistic appeal. The chief grievance of the Welsh farmer was the tithe to support an 'alien' Church or (worse still), anglicized landlords whose forbears had appropriated it. In 1886 there erupted a 'tithe war' in which farmers forcibly resisted attempts to dis-

Tithe disturbances, Denbigh, 1890

Victorian farm kitchen (Llwyn Celyn, Llanberis)

train on the stock of defaulters. The disturbances were concentrated in the vale of Clwyd, where troops had to be drafted in; but the whole countryside was in turmoil, and eventually the law was modified to hold the landlord, not the tenant, directly responsible for the payment of tithe. But a quarter of a century passed before disestablishment reached the statute book, and

almost another decade before it became effective. By that time
interest in what had been the most bitterly divisive force in
Welsh life since the Restoration, had largely evaporated.

Another issue in which the Irish example played its part was
the land question. Ireland had been an awful warning in the
days of the enclosure movement, when allotments for cottagers
were in question; now the enfranchised cottager turned the

tables on the landlord by demanding the security of tenure and facilities for purchase by which Gladstone was unsuccessfully trying to solve the Irish question. But the Welsh landlord, if anglicized, was neither absentee nor alien, nor was the Welsh peasant as downtrodden as the Irish; it was not till 1894 that Gladstone consented to appoint a royal commission on Welsh land. Its massive report had no practical effect, for when it appeared in 1896 Gladstone was in retirement, the Liberals in the wilderness, and agriculture momentarily on the up-grade.

In the sphere of education the appeal to Irish precedents proved more fruitful. Irish education at all levels had benefited in recent years from exchequer grants. Wales still had to rely on self-help save for elementary education (where the bulk of the money still went to church schools) and the training of the Anglican clergy; but in 1880 Gladstone accepted the recommendation of a departmental committee for exchequer grants to support two colleges for North and South Wales respectively;

An impoverished Carmarthenshire farm, Blaenwaun, Llansadwrn

to these was later added a further grant to the existing institution at Aberystwyth, which for twelve years had maintained itself on voluntary contributions. Not until Gladstone's last ministry were the colleges federated into a degree-giving university; meanwhile Welsh education had been made less top-heavy by implementing the other main recommendation of the departmental committee—state-aided secondary schools. The concept of Wales as a distinct entity, with her own claims on the legislature, had taken firm root, irrespective of the government in power.

The struggle for Irish Home Rule both stimulated the milder national ambitions of Wales and provided her with useful lessons in political pressure. By 1888 the Welsh leaders who had risen to prominence since 1830—most of them self-educated men—were quitting the scene; their place was being taken by a younger generation, several fresh from the university. The youngest—Thomas Ellis, a Merioneth Methodist farmer's son—came to Parliament fortified with a burning zeal against agrarian tyranny and a conviction that the self-determination for which the Irish peasant was fighting was also the answer for his Welsh counterpart.

It was this group which formed in 1886 the *Cymru Fydd* ('Wales-to-be') movement, designed to work within the Liberal framework for a Welsh version of Home Rule. In the preceding year the Society for Utilising the Welsh Language had set out to safeguard this heritage in elementary education; within a few years it had succeeded in forcing the acceptance of Welsh as a teaching subject in the schools and training colleges. In Parliament the Welsh Liberals, reinforced from 1891 by the young David Lloyd George, acted as a party within a party; but the older Gladstonians restrained those who itched to become an independent Welsh Home Rule party, and Ellis himself accepted office under Gladstone.

During this period relations between Church and Chapel were brought to a bitter climax by the oratorical campaigns of Lloyd George and the politicians on one side, and the Church Defence League, led by the bishops of St Asaph and St David's, on the other. A new bone of contention was introduced by the Education Act of 1902, which placed Church

The earliest Punch *cartoon of Lloyd George, 1900*

schools on the rates and provoked the Passive Resistance movement of the Nonconformists. For years the tendency in all public appointments was to place qualifications second to religious and political affiliations — an unedifying chapter in Welsh history. On the other hand, the ceremonial investiture in 1911 of the Prince of Wales (the future Edward VIII) brought together the radical politician and the militant bishop of St Asaph, who were its principal sponsors, and provided a welcome lull in the storms of politics and religion.

The prolongation into the industrial age of a radicalism based on the preoccupations of rural Nonconformity — the fight against privilege, attachment to the soil and to a language and traditions beginning to lose ground in the towns, and a countryman's inbred hatred of militarism — is not easy to explain. Perhaps the most important factor was the Welsh-language denominational press, which from mid-century had been giving more attention to political issues. The editors, nearly all of them Nonconformists well-known as preachers and lecturers, wrote on a wide range of subjects; and over most of Wales, where English newspapers still had little circulation, these journals provided the political education of an increasingly literate population.

By the turn of the century the tone was changing. Industrial relations were becoming more embittered, and industrial Wales was beginning to shake off both rural ideologies and middle-class leadership. In 1886 Mabon and W. J. Parry were elected to represent Wales in the Labour Electoral Committee appointed by the Trade Union Congress to pursue the Chartist aim of working-class representation in Parliament. In the same year the succession of a new Lord Penrhyn bent on smashing the quarrymen's union led to a stoppage of nearly a year in 1896–7, and in 1900 a second which, with help from outside sympathizers, was kept going for three years, leaving a permanently crippled industry; by 1914 employment in it was down to half what it had been before the strike.

Meanwhile, in 1898, a six months' strike had closed half the pits of South Wales, and although at its close Mabon was elected president of the South Wales Miners' Federation, his conciliatory leadership was bitterly challenged. At the 'khaki' election two years later Merthyr made history by electing, as running-mate to the Liberal mineowner who had represented it since 1888, the Scottish ex-miner Keir Hardie, chairman of the Independent Labour Party. Industrial Wales was beginning to take the bit between its teeth.

With the collapse of the *Cymru Fydd* movement in 1895, Welsh nationalism soft-pedalled its political aims and returned for thirty years to its cultural bases. The university colleges helped to give a firmer foundation to Welsh language and history. Literature, both poetry and prose, branched out in many directions, and a succession of Welsh-language periodi-

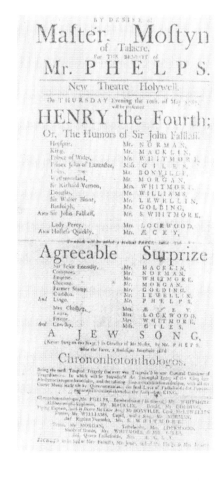

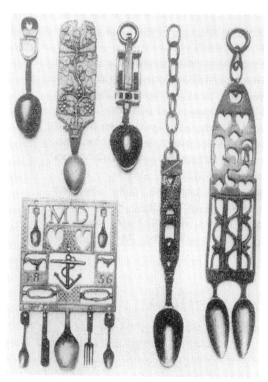

Love spoons (Llwyau serch)

cals concerned less with politics than with literature, philosophy and theology diffused a critical sense and a wider acquaintance with European thought. But in a country with a denationalized gentry and weak in urban development, the fine arts had little scope. Drama, once the *anterliwt* had fallen into disrepute, depended on occasional visits of English touring companies, usually under the patronage of the gentry, and these declined as the gentry lost interest.

The musical talents of the people found vent in choral singing, with the limited *repertoire* of chapel, quarry or colliery choirs. Folk song, as elsewhere, was in decline, but the early years of Victoria saw the first systematic effort to collect what survived. No painter of note had appeared in Wales since the eighteenth century, when Richard Wilson found his way to fame. Since then any artistic bent had to express itself in country crafts like the wooden 'love spoons', which a young man would fashion for his lady-love. In the first few decades of the twentieth century individual artistic patronage was giving way to collective effort, to which both university and eisteddfod contributed.

Early in the new century Wales was convulsed by the religious revival of 1904–5, the first for fifty years; for nine months it drew crowds away from Rugby matches and forced publicans to put up their shutters. Since its impact was mainly on Nonconformists and non-churchgoers, it did nothing to mend the political and religious rifts in the community, but it generated a mood of spiritual exaltation which contributed to the fervour of Liberal meetings when the election came next winter. In the new Parliament Keir Hardie was one of six Welsh members returned under independent Labour colours, but the Liberals made a clean sweep of the rest of the country. The mantle of Ellis now fell on Lloyd George, who was increasingly absorbed in English politics. Welsh Home Rule was whittled down to the creation of a Welsh department of the Board of Education, an important concession for those who had been championing the cause of Welsh in the schools. National pride was further gratified by the foundation of the National Library at Aberystwyth and the National Museum at Cardiff. Pressure from Welsh M.P.s procured the charters, but private generosity made them living institutions—whether from wealthy donors providing sites or priceless exhibits, or humbler subscribers. These two great institutions—like their predecessors the university colleges—were more impressive monuments to Welsh nationhood than any political achievement.

The outbreak of war in 1914 brought this creative period to an end, shattered many illusions, and opened a new chapter in Welsh history whose trend, even after half a century, is still not easy to discern.

Further Reading

R. T. Jenkins and H. Ramage, *History of the Hon. Society of Cymmrodorion* (*Y Cymmrodor, L*), 1951.

E. T. Davies, *Religion and the Industrial Revolution in South Wales*, 1965.

D. Attwater, *The Catholic Church in Modern Wales*, 1935.

David Williams, 'Chartism in Wales', in Asa Briggs (ed.), *Chartist Studies*, 1959.

Id., *The Rebecca Riots: a Study in Agrarian Discontent*, 1955.

Report of Commission of Enquiry into the State of Education in Wales (3 vols.), 1847.

E. D. Lewis, *The Rhondda Valleys*, 1959.

E. W. Evans, *The Miners of South Wales*, 1961.

Epilogue:

Wales since 1914

The outbreak of war came as a profound shock to the pacifist sentiment which had spread through Wales since the days of Henry Richard, and had risen to the surface again during the Boer War, with Lloyd George as one of its chief protagonists. But the slogan 'Gallant Little Belgium' carried an obvious appeal to the smaller nations. Units of the historic Welsh regiments, and even some of their younger territorial battalions, were in action during the first months of war, and the recruitment of 'Kitchener's Army' brought in volunteers from every walk of life, till by the end of 1915 Wales had fifty thousand men in the field or in training, including the newly-formed Welsh Guards.

All this was accompanied by a vast expansion of the heavy industries of the south, with high wages and full employment. In the northern counties, makers of agricultural machinery metaphorically turned ploughshares into swords; even the lead and textile industries were galvanized into activity, and as food shortages began to loom, agriculture enjoyed a prosperity unequalled since the Napoleonic Wars. On the other hand, the decline of the slate industry was hastened by the halt in building and the resort to cheaper materials. A striking novelty was the widespread entry of women into industry. On small farms they had always worked with the family, but the Land Army recruited them for more general agricultural service; still more revolutionary was their employment—up to eighty per cent of the total labour force—in munitions; for women had not been employed in the heavy industries for two generations, and their employment in textiles had shrunk with the decline of the Welsh industry.

South Wales unemployed miners singing outside a London theatre, 1932

With the return of peace this artificial expansion came to an abrupt stop. South Wales was the hardest hit. Not only was the demand for iron, steel and tinplate drastically reduced, but even coal exports, on which the region had come to depend, sank disastrously. As long as the war lasted, the slump in exports was masked by the inflated demands of the munitions industry; but their withdrawal revealed the nakedness of the land. The South American market had already been captured by the United States, and the coal requirements of France, on which Cardiff had prospered for sixty years, were now met by the reparations imposed on Germany. By 1932 unemployment in Wales—concentrated mainly in the south—had reached nearly a quarter of a million out of a total population of a million and a half. South Wales was designated a Special Area, and public and private efforts were directed to the planting of new industries. But during the first decade of peace nearly 260,000 of the more able-bodied and enterprising migrated to the English industrial districts, while at home a generation was growing up which had never known regular employment.

In rural Wales the effects were less spectacular but no less disquieting. The agricultural boom collapsed when the stimulus of the Corn Production Act was withdrawn; cultivation receded as it had done after 1815, and farmers turned to milk production for the big towns and the manufacturers of synthetic foodstuffs. As motor traffic became common, the rough platform at the entrance to the farm track, with its half-dozen milk containers awaiting the early morning visit of the motor lorry, became a familiar feature of the landscape. But milk production, as it became mechanized, called for fewer hands, and rural Wales was also caught in the depressing fog of unemployment and depopulation.

All this reawakened fears for the future of the language. With the continual growth of population till 1931, the number who counted themselves Welsh-speaking increased also, but in diminishing proportions, till in 1921 there began a positive decline; by then not much more than a third of the inhabitants used the language, as against some sixty per cent when the century opened. There were of course wide local variations, ranging from eighty per cent in the more rural westerly shires to five or six in the south-eastern borderland. To arrest the drift there was founded in 1922 the Welsh League of Youth (*Urdd Gobaith Cymru*), with its annual camps, sports (*mabolgampau*) and eisteddfodau. A report issued in 1927 from the Board of Education, after analysing the historical background of the problem, outlined an enlightened programme of bilingual education in the schools, and largely determined the lines of development since then.

Other efforts took a more political, and sometimes less peaceable form. The fact that Ireland had now won her independence was not lost on Wales. The foundation of the *Urdd* was followed by that of the Welsh National Party (*Y Blaid Genedlaethol Cymru*) with aims like those embodied in the treaty negotiated by Lloyd George with the Irish leaders. Even the violence in which Ireland had been engulfed had its pale reflection in the action of three leaders of the Blaid when in 1936, on principles which were a blend of pacifism and nationalism, they set fire to Air Force installations under construction in Caernarvonshire. Their trial provided them with a forum for urging the legal claims of the Welsh language, and their protest may have helped to hasten the repeal of the 'language' clauses of the Act of Union four years later; but a whole generation passed before their party returned its first (and so far its only) member to parliament.

This upsurge of nationalism was mainly a rural phenomenon; for industrial Wales bread-and-butter questions were more immediate. The political legacy of the Depression was the rise of the Labour party, which by 1929 had increased its Welsh representation from six to twenty-five, leaving the rural areas as the last refuge of Nonconformist Liberalism. Trade unionism, with the official status conferred on it by the war, grew rapidly, even extending to agricultural labour; and the Welsh unions were swallowed up by those great national aggregations which have become the mainstay of Labour politics. The South Wales miners had long been part of a nationwide federation which became affiliated to the Labour party; the North Wales quarrymen were more reluctant to jettison their traditional Liberal loyalties, but in 1922 they were absorbed into the Transport and General Workers' Union: the 'industrial isolationism' of Wales was 'withering away'.

Then came the Second World War, with its fresh crop of casualties, extending now to the home front in the three-night bombing of Swansea. Unemployment again ceased to trouble; instead came direction of labour, bringing 'Bevin boys' into the depleted Welsh pits and drafting men from less essential industries (like slate quarrying) into the war effort, whether in industrial Wales or across the border. To add to the dislocation of rural Wales, much of it was designated a 'reception area' for evacuees from threatened English cities. At the same time restrictions on travel, and the dangers involved in large crowds, reduced to a shadow the national eisteddfod, which in the First World War had contributed to morale and had evoked some of the finest oratorical flights of Lloyd George. That the institution was kept alive at all was a triumph of patriotic zeal; so too was the free distribution to Welshmen in the forces and in English munition works of a monthly Welsh news sheet, *Cofion Cymru*, compiled, printed and distributed by a small band of enthusiasts intent on keeping these exiles in touch with their homeland and their mother-tongue.

Nationalism took on a new face again after the war. Not only did Plaid Cymru extend its membership and increase its polls, but impatience at its failure to achieve tangible results led to the emergence of small but demonstrative bodies disposed to reject the slow processes of parliamentary democracy. Direct action took a variety of forms, from 'sit-downs' and daubing of slogans, through the courting of prison sentences by refusal to fill in official forms in English, to deadlier affrays like the use of plastic bombs. Apart from the language question, these demonstrations have been directed against the diversion to English cities of precious Welsh water supplies and (more recently) against the revival of the investiture ceremony of 1911 in respect of another 'English' Prince of Wales—though this time one who can use the language of his Principality with fluency and wit.

More constructively, a good deal has been achieved during the post-war period towards strengthening the legal basis of Welsh nationhood. The creation of a Welsh Office, centred in Cardiff, with control over widening areas of Welsh life and with responsible spokesmen in the government, has brought the status of Wales more into line with that of Scotland; and two successive reports on the language have made recommendations, gradually coming into effect, designed to consolidate its formal standing. Persistent pressure has also blunted the threat to the language through broadcasting, by the establishment of an autonomous Welsh district with programmes in the two tongues. In other respects social change in Wales during the past fifty or sixty years, whether directly due to wartime pressures or not, has been part of a wider pattern: the desertion of the country house, the decline of habits of church-going and of traditional moralities; above all, the spread of a cosmopolitan culture in recreation and educational method, in architecture and in popular music. How far the historic character of life in Wales will be able to hold its own against these currents only the future can show.

INDEX

INDEX

INDEX

INDEX

INDEX

SELECT BIBLIOGRAPHY

John Davies	*History of Wales*	1994
John Davies	*The Making of Wales*	1996
Gwyn A. Williams	*When was Wales?*	1979
Wendy Davies	*Wales in the Early Middle Ages*	1982
R. R. Davies	*The Age of Conquest: Wales 1063-1415*	1991
David Walker	*Medieval Wales*	1990
A. D. Carr	*Medieval Wales*	1995
R. R. Davies	*The Revolt of Owain Glyn Dŵr*	1995
Glanmor Williams	*Renewal and Reformation: Wales c.1415-1642*	1993
J. Gwynfor Jones	*Early Modern Wales 1525-1640*	1994
G. H. Jenkins	*The Foundations of Modern Wales*	1987
G. Elwyn Jones	*Modern Wales: a concise history c.1485-1979*	1984
Philip Jenkins	*A History of Modern Wales 1536-1990*	1992
K. O. Morgan	*Rebirth of a Nation 1880-1980*	1981

A.D.C.
1998

Further Reading

A. J. Lush, *The Young Adult in South Wales*, 1941.
C. Parry, *The Radical Tradition in Welsh Politics*, 1970.
Welsh in Education and in Life, Report to Board of Education, 1927.
G. Morgan, *The Dragon's Tongue*, 1966.